IRELAND
People and Places

St. Patrick's Day Parade, Dublin

IRELAND

People and Places

A CELEBRATION OF
IRELAND'S CULTURAL HERITAGE

Dáithí Ó hÓgáin

Fishing on the River Boyne

SALAMANDER

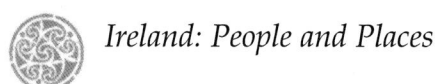

A Salamander Book

Published by Salamander Books Ltd.
8 Blenheim Court
Brewery Road
London N7 9NY

© Salamander Books Ltd., 2003

A member of **Chrysalis** Books plc

ISBN 1 84065 362 0

All correspondence concerning the content of this volume should be addressed to Salamander Books Ltd.

The Author

Dáithí Ó hÓgáin, MA, PhD, is Associate Professor at University College Dublin, Ireland, where he lectures on Irish folklore. He is the author of over 20 books, several of them in Irish, on aspects of folk culture, history and tradition. He is also a noted poet and short-story writer, and is a well-known conference lecturer. He has participated in the production of documentary films in Europe and the United States, and is a frequent TV and radio broadcaster.

Credits

Project Manager: Ray Bonds
Designer: Heather Moore, Mitchell Print and Publishing Solutions
Picture researcher: Brian Kelly
Colour reproduction: Anorax, UK
Printed in Italy by G. Canale & C.

Sybil Point, County Kerry

Contents

Introduction • 8

Connacht • 12
Keshcorran, County Sligo 14 • Rathcroghan, County Roscommon 17 • Castle on Clare Island, County Mayo 18 • Galway Hookers 21 • Fleadh Cheoil na hÉireann 22 • Cruises on the River Shannon 24

Leinster • 26
St. Brigid's Cathedral, Kildare 29 • Horse-racing at Punchestown, County Kildare 30 • The Great Sugarloaf, County Wicklow 33 • Avondale House, County Wicklow 34 • Effigies in St. Canice's Cathedral, Kilkenny 37 • Blackstairs Mountains, Counties Wexford and Carlow 38 • Kilmore Quay, County Wexford 41 • Loftus Hall, Fethard-on-Sea, County Wexford 42 • Pleasure in Pubs, Dublin 45 • St. Patrick's Cathedral, Dublin 46 • St. Patrick's Day Parade, Dublin 48 • Hurling at Croke Park, Dublin 50 • Dublin Castle, Dublin 53 • The Tomb of Strongbow, Christchurch, Dublin 54 • The Mansion House, Dublin 57 • St. Enda's Museum, Dublin 58 • The Guinness Brewery, Dublin 60 • River Boyne 62 • Lia Fáil Stone, County Meath 65 • Athlone, County Westmeath 66 • Ardee, County Louth 69

Ulster • 70
Mountsandel, County Derry 73 • Sheep-fair, Draperstown, County Derry 74 • Tory Island, County Donegal 77 • Killybegs Harbour, County Donegal 78 • Tullaghogue, County Tyrone 81 • Cave Hill, County Antrim, 82 • Orange Parade, County Down 85 • Dundrum Bay, County Down 86 • Loughbrickland, County Down 88 • The Kavanagh Museum, Inniskeen, County Monaghan 91 • Mummers 92 • Bowling, County Armagh 95

Munster • 96
The Burren, County Clare 99 • Kincora, Killaloe, County Clare 100 • Spanish Point, County Clare 103 • Scattery Island, County Clare 104 • Knockfeerina, County Limerick 107 • Ballyneety, Pallasgreen, County Limerick 108 • The Collegiate Church, Kilmallock, County Limerick 111 • The De Valera Museum, Bruree, County Limerick 112 • Sybil Point, County Kerry 115 • Ross Castle, County Kerry 116 • Recreated Bogland Village, Glenbeigh, County Kerry 119 • Kenmare Bay, County Kerry 120 • Gougane Barra, County Cork 123 • The Old Head of Kinsale, County Cork 124 • The 'Moving Statue' at Ballinspittle, County Cork 127 • Blarney Castle, County Cork 128 • Horse-fair at Cahirmee, County Cork 131 • Tountinna, County Tipperary 132 • Mount Bruis, Shronell, County Tipperary 135 • Crotty's Rock, County Waterford 136 • Wren-boys 139

Picture Credits • 140
Index • 142

The Burren, County Clare.

Introduction

Geographical location is one of the great determining factors in our lives, affecting not only economic and social issues but even our speech, attitudes, and traditions. Conversely, the activities of people play a major, often crucial, role in shaping the environment. This interplay between people and places can perhaps be best expressed by defining culture simply as how we come to terms with our surroundings – a process easily discernible in public terms, but which is just as real in the inner aesthetic feelings which to a greater or less extent are experienced by every individual.

I live in Bray, a pleasant seaside town in County Wicklow, and a wise man of this town told me a story which I think has relevance here. Hundreds of years ago, he said, a young man of the place was walking one day near to where the river Dargle meets the sea. The young man was surprised to see a beautiful sailing ship gliding in to shore, and he was even more surprised when he was welcomed aboard to partake of some refreshment. He did not hesitate, and as he drank with his new-found companions they invited him to come with them to see the world. Again he assented, and the ship sailed out of the little harbour, into the Irish Sea, and from there sailed into all the seas of the world. Travelling on and on, and stopping for a while in many lands, the young man experienced all the various climes, met many different peoples, saw all the styles of buildings and the designs of cities.

He was so fascinated by his travels, so full of the vigour of youth, that he did not feel the passage of time, until one

Strawboys in Kerry: Irish festival disguise is a journey into the realm of fancy.

Bray Head and seafront, County Wicklow.

day he grew homesick and enquired about some ship which might perhaps be heading towards Ireland again. He eventually found one, and so he was brought back once more to the mouth of the river Dargle. As he stepped ashore, he looked all around in expectation, but a strange sensation came over him. Yes, the countryside was the same as before, with the winding river and the long extended hills, but all else was different. The fine new town of Bray had grown up, with roadways and bridges and railway, houses and shops and hotels. It was then that he realised that his trip abroad had been a magical one, in the company of timeless sailors on the timeless sea, and that hundreds of years had passed unnoticed by him.

Unlike many other stories of this type, it is not specified here whether the character became an old, wizened man upon stepping ashore or whether he embraced with great enthusiasm the new surroundings. It would have depended, I suppose, on which was more important to him – the unchanged or the changed. But this is just a story and, in reality, the opposition between these two is never so stark, for the sense of place depends on our own perspective, on the vistas of our world as seen through human eyes and lived through human experience. This book has many examples of what was and what is – of people in action and people imagining, of life coming to places and of places coming to life....

— **Dáithí Ó hÓgáin**

CONNACHT

Midsummer bonfire near the beach at Rossport, County Mayo.
This old custom survives strongly in the west of Ireland.

Keshcorran

County Sligo

In the south-east of County Sligo lies a broad mountain, nearly four and a half miles (7 kilometres) in circumference. On its summit – 1,180 feet (360 metres) high – prehistoric people constructed a large burial-cairn and enclosure. The origin of its name, *Ceis Chorainn*, is obscure, but *ceis* probably meant 'circuit' and the toponymic Corann may have been derived from an old population name. Mediaeval authors fancied that a fairy musician called Corann lived there and had a wonderful harp (*céis*). More wondrous still is the natural formation of the western side of the mountain, where seventeen caves stand like portals of a great geological terrace. Remains of many prehistoric animals have been found in these caves, including bears, Irish elk, reindeer, and even lemmings. Humans once lived in these caves also, and one of them is cited in Old Irish literature as the place where the mythical king Cormac Mac Airt was suckled by a she-wolf as a child.

When the hero Fionn Mac Cumhaill and his men rested on top of the mountain after a great deer-hunt, the otherworld lord of the mountain, Conarán, sent his three witch daughters to capture them. The three placed iron-bands around three briar-trunks and began to twist the bands withershins. Seeing the horrid appearance of the witches and mesmerised by their ritual, Fionn and his men changed complexion from red to white and then black, before collapsing onto the ground. They were tied up, and brought into the otherworld residence. Fionn's lieutenant, Goll Mac Morna, arriving late for the hunt, became suspicious and he engaged the witches in combat. He slew two of them, and forced the other to unbind the spell on his friends. Fionn was so grateful that he gave his daughter in marriage to Goll on that very day.

The great sombre terrace in the mountainside.

RATHCROHAN

The burial place of the kings of Connaught covers an area of 518 hectares. There are more than 20 ring forts, burial mounds and megalithic tombs, principally Relig na Rí (burial ground of the kings), Rath na dTarbh (fort of the bulls) and Rathbeg. Unfortunately because the earthworks are so spread out over a huge area, apart from a 2m high standing stone said to mark the grave of King Dathí, last pagan King of Ireland, even a trained eye finds it difficult to make sense of the site. This area is the setting for the tragedy and the bloody conclusion of the epic Táin Bo

Rathcroghan
County Roscommon

Between the towns of Tulsk and Bellanagare, in County Roscommon, lies a crossroads which is surrounded by a large complex of tumuli, ringforts, enclosures, and monoliths. The general area is known as *Cruachain* ('place of mounds'), and its focus is a large, flat-topped tumulus, some 13 feet (4 metres) high and with a diameter of about 290 feet (88 metres). This is called *Ráth Chruachna* ('the fort of Cruachain'), and until the end of the Middle Ages it was the assembly-place of the O'Connor kings. These O'Connors were descendants of the ruling tribe of Tara in the 5th century AD, the Connachta, and it was their presence west of the Shannon which caused that province to be known as Connacht.

The founder of their kingship was Nath Í – nephew of the great Tara king, Niall – and a mound about half a mile south of Rathcroghan, with a pillarstone on top, is claimed as his burial-place. Most dramatic of all was the early transference from Tara to Rathcroghan of the mythology associated with the goddess of sovereignty, Meadhbh (earlier *Meduva*, 'the intoxicating one'). In humanising her, the storytellers said that she was a Tara princess who married the reigning king of the area, Ailill, but that she was scheming and ambitious and had many other lovers besides. Between Rathcroghan and the mound of Nath Í, slightly to the west, is a natural cave with a man-built entrance. It is called *Uaimh na gCat* ('cave of the cats'). This was believed to be an entrance to the otherworld, being guarded by fierce cats which attacked any live warrior who entered. An inscription on a roof-stone in the cave mentions a 'son of Meduva' – this dates to the late 6th century, and shows that the cult of the mother-goddess was established at that time in this quiet place.

Castle on Clare Island

County Mayo

Guarding the mouth of Clew Bay, and facing the Atlantic, is the mountainous Clare Island. This was a stronghold of the powerful O'Malley clan, and the ruins of their castle overlook the harbour there. The castle was built in the early 16th century, but was modernised in 1831 for use as a coastguard station. Popular tradition associates it with the famous pirate-queen of the O'Malley family, Gráinne Mhaol (c1530-1603). Her name means 'Grace the Obtuse', and she was married twice – first to a chieftain of the O'Flahertys and then to Sir Richard Burke.

Gráinne had a small fleet of swift ships and, during her long and eventful career, she raided along the west coast of Ireland and even as far as Scotland. Carefully avoiding taking any side in the wars of that time, she suffered no discomfiture from these except for short stays in prison in Limerick and Dublin. Folklore retains many accounts of her raids and daring. It is said that she gave birth to her son, Theobald Burke, while on board one of her ships. The ship was attacked that very day by a Turkish corsair, and Gráinne jumped up out of bed and went on deck firing two blunderbusses. The Turks were so taken aback by the sight that Gráinne's men gained the advantage over them and won the victory. To stop English attacks on her Mayo strongholds, she sailed to London in 1593 and had an interview with Queen Elizabeth. It is said that, having used her handkerchief, Gráinne threw it into the fire and, when queried on this by the queen, she remarked that Irish ladies were much too sophisticated to return such a used item to their pocket!

The restored castle facing the mainland.

Galway Hookers

Alarge variety of boats are used in Ireland. Museums show some timber dug-out examples from prehistoric times, but from an early date the type of rowing boat called *curach* has been more popular. The original meaning of *curach* was 'construct', and it consists of a light framework of timber laths. The boat was rendered waterproof by a covering of ox-skins, but in recent centuries this has been replaced by tarred canvas. These little boats – with benches for two to four rowers – have proved very suitable for fishing on the Atlantic coast. There are local variations in design, all the way from the small Donegal versions to the long and very sleek version in west Kerry called a *naomhóg*.

Small sailing boats were preferred along the east coast of Ireland, and for more extended travel a special type was developed in the 17th century. This was known as the 'hooker' and seems to have been influenced by similar craft used in Holland. Although the hooker spread rapidly through Irish ports, it was in time superseded by newer and larger boats, and the only examples still in use are to be found on the Galway coast. A Galway hooker may be up to 46 feet (14 metres) in length, being about twice the size of a *curach* and many times heavier. Built locally from larched planks on sawn oak frames, it is fitted with mainsail, foresail, and jib. It has a high rounded bow, and is usually manned by a crew of two. Its traditional purpose was fishing and delivering cargo – especially turf and animals – along the extensive Galway coastline, but nowadays it is used more for pleasure and sport. Regattas are held regularly, and races between hookers draw a large and excited crowd of spectators.

The Irish people have always loved music. There are archaeological finds of trumpets, horns, and hand-bells from as early as the Bronze Age, but the most popular Irish instrument in antiquity was the harp. This was strung with brass wires and plucked with the fingernails, and was played at feasts and assemblies. A smaller stringed instrument, played with both bow and plectrum, was called a *tiompán*. There was also the simple pipe, as well as the large wooden bag-pipe used to stir up the spirit of warriors in battle. It was said that expert musicians had magical power and could play three special strains – one to soothe listeners to sleep, one to make them sorrowful, and one to create mirth.

For several centuries now, the elbow (*uillinn*) pipes, played from a seated position, have been most popular. Other instruments have been adopted from abroad and have become great mainstays of traditional music. These include flutes, accordians and violins, while simpler and more spontaneous ways of keeping rhythm such as a little drum (*bodhrán*), a set of spoons, and 'mouth-music' have long been in use. The Irish ways of singing and making music break down into two basic categories – plaintive slow airs on the one hand, and fast exuberant airs on the other. A music festival is called a *fleadh cheoil*, and there are many such local festivals under the auspices of Comhaltas Ceoltóirí Éireann, an organisation with over 400 branches spread throughout Ireland and abroad. The local festivals culminate in the great annual *Fleadh Cheoil*, held at a different venue each year. The attendance well exceeds 200,000 people, making it the largest single social event in the Irish calendar.

Fleadh Cheoil na hÉireann

(National Music Festival)

Cruises on the River Shannon

(various counties)

The greatest of Irish rivers, the Shannon touches on all four provinces of the country. It rises in the Cuilcagh Mountains in Ulster, its banks for a long distance form the boundary between Connacht and Leinster, and it finally enters the sea through its large estuary in the west of Munster. Its full length is 241 miles (386 kilometres), and in its waters there are many small islands, some of which were inhabited until recent times. It is still home to many salmon farms as well as to the huge hydroelectric station at Ardnacrusha in County Clare. The river is navigable as far as Limerick, and is the reason why that city has historically been one of the most important of Irish ports. The praises of this river have been sung by many poets, and a cruise on the Shannon – with the wild beauty of Connacht on its western shoreline – is a most pleasurable experience.

The river's name in Irish is *Sionainn*, a title deriving from the ancient Celtic *Senona* with the meaning of 'revered old lady'. This represents the very ancient tradition of regarding rivers as female, symbolical of the life-giving and wise goddess, and it is clear that this river was considered synonymous with the great ancestral mother on whom the welfare of the Irish depended. Using echoes from ancient tradition, the mediaeval poets invented a tragic story. According to it, Sionainn was the name of a beautiful, golden-haired maiden who once noticed bright bubbles in the river. Believing that these bubbles contained wisdom, she waded through the water in an attempt to reach them, but she was drowned, and ever after the river bears her name.

LEINSTER

*The Grand Canal in Dublin – a strong imprint of human
hands, stretching through much of the province.*

St. Brigid's Cathedral

Kildare

Towards the end of the 5th century, a holy woman from a subject tribe came to a pagan sanctuary in the middle of Leinster and converted it to Christianity. Because a great oak-tree grew there, the place became known as *Cill Dara* ('church of the oak'). The holy woman herself was given the title which belonged to the priestess of the sanctuary – *Brigid*, which meant 'highest one' – and by that name she is known to posterity. The foundation of St. Brigid was unique in early Ireland in that it contained two monasteries, one for women and one for men. The earliest remains on the present site, however, belong to the Middle Ages, and were subject to drastic restoration in the 19th century. Of special interest are the fine effigies within the cathedral, and in the grounds an old granite high cross and a refashioned round tower almost 110 feet (33 metres) high.

Devotion to St. Brigid – originally the special patroness of Leinster – spread rapidly throughout Ireland and Scotland. She shared her name with a well-known Celtic goddess, and as a result the saint was invested with all the nurturing faculties of such a personage. Her feastday, February 1, is the beginning of spring and coincides with the ancient festival which was called *Oímelg* ('lactation'). She is therefore considered the protectress of calves and lambs in particular, and of agricultural work in general. Special St. Brigid's Crosses are woven from rushes and are hung in houses and cow-byres so as to ensure health and good fortune. The design of these varies from region to region – they include crosses with single or multiple lozenge shapes, crosses with unaligned arms, crosses within circles, and more simple three-legged crosses.

Horse-racing at Punchestown

County Kildare

The Celtic god Lugus, known as Lugh in Irish tradition, was patron of the harvest festival, and the ancient Irish claimed that he was the originator of horse-racing. The famous racing festival at Galway is still held at his festival, *Lughnasa*, the beginning of autumn, and it attracts large crowds and great celebration. The prevailing festive spirit of that season can therefore be seen as a survival of what was once regarded as a sacred activity. One of the favourite places for this exalted pastime was the plain of Kildare, which has been known since antiquity as the *Currach*, an ancient Irish word which meant simply 'racecourse'. Since the 18th century modern racing has been held there – particularly in summer – and it is now one of the most celebrated centres for flat-racing in the world.

A few miles to the east of the Curragh lies another racecourse, at Punchestown, but this course is famous for steeplechasing in the spring. It is said that this form of racing originated in County Cork, when in the year 1752 two riders competed with each other in a race from the church at Buttevant to the steeple of St. Leger, a distance of about four-and-a-quarter miles (7 kilometres). The idea was to race cross-country, the horses being ridden over every obstacle in the way. Modern steeplechasing, of course, takes place on a set course, and the obstacles may be fences of brush or timber, with a water-jump sometimes included. Punchestown preserves one example of another type of obstacle once found on many local Irish racecourses. This is a large, flat-topped bank on which the horses land before jumping down off it again and racing on at full speed.

Take-off at the bank.

The Great Sugarloaf
County Wicklow

This cone-shaped mountain towers to a height of 165 feet (504 metres), over land and sea. It is easily climbed, apart from the final stage, and has a flat top from which a tremendous view can be had of the surrounding plain of north Wicklow. Its name in English dates from the 17th century, and is due to its white appearance. In Irish it is known as *Sliabh Chualann*, meaning the mountain of the Cualainn, an ancient Celtic tribe which inhabited this whole area. A variant name replaced the word *Sliabh* with *Oe* ('an ear'), because of its shape like an animal's ear, and it was fancifully said to have been the listening-post of the Cualainn as they protected their territory from enemies.

According to myth, the great father-deity of the Irish, called the Daghdha, having been inveigled out of his residence at the tumulus of Newgrange in County Meath, had a palace constructed for himself on the top of this mountain. Sliabh Chualann was anciently a focus for assemblies and fairs, and a tradition – fostered by some class-conscious druids – pointed to it as the symbol of an ordered society. The aristocracy and the common people should not be mixed, it was claimed, just as the heather which grows at the foot of this mountain never reaches to the clear white top on which choice flowers grow. The view which generally prevailed in early Ireland, however, was that 'a man is better than his birth'. It only took five generations, it was said, for a king's descendants to sink to poverty, or for a beggar's to rise to kingship.

The mountain stands as a sentinel.

Avondale House
County Wicklow

Referred to in a patriotic ballad as 'the Blackbird of sweet Avondale', Charles Stewart Parnell (1846-1891) was one of the most brilliant and romantic figures in Irish political history. His residence was Avondale House, just over a mile (2 kilometres) to the south of the village of Rathdrum. Built in 1779, it has a two-storey hall with a gallery, and contains some fine plasterwork. The house is now a museum, devoted to Parnell's life and career, and the surrounding estate is a forestry park and college, with specimens of plants from many parts of the world.

The son of a liberal landlord and a radical American mother, from his youth Parnell sympathised with the Irish people in the oppression which they suffered. He joined the Home Rule party and was elected to the Westminster Parliament in 1875. Two years later he became leader of that party, and skilfully took advantage of the ongoing struggle for power in Parliament between the Liberals and Conservatives. By 1879, his leadership qualities were so obvious that he was referred to as 'the uncrowned king of Ireland'. He gave his support to the Land League, which sought to break the power of landlordism, and this caused him to be accused of incitement to violence. He was jailed in 1881, but the British Government felt compelled to release him, and his influence was at its zenith in 1890 when it became known that he was having an affair with a married woman, Mrs Kitty O'Shea. Political opportunism and sectarian feeling conspired against Ireland's great Protestant patriot, and his party was split. He worked feverishly to save the cause of Home Rule, but his over-exertions led to health failure and a premature death.

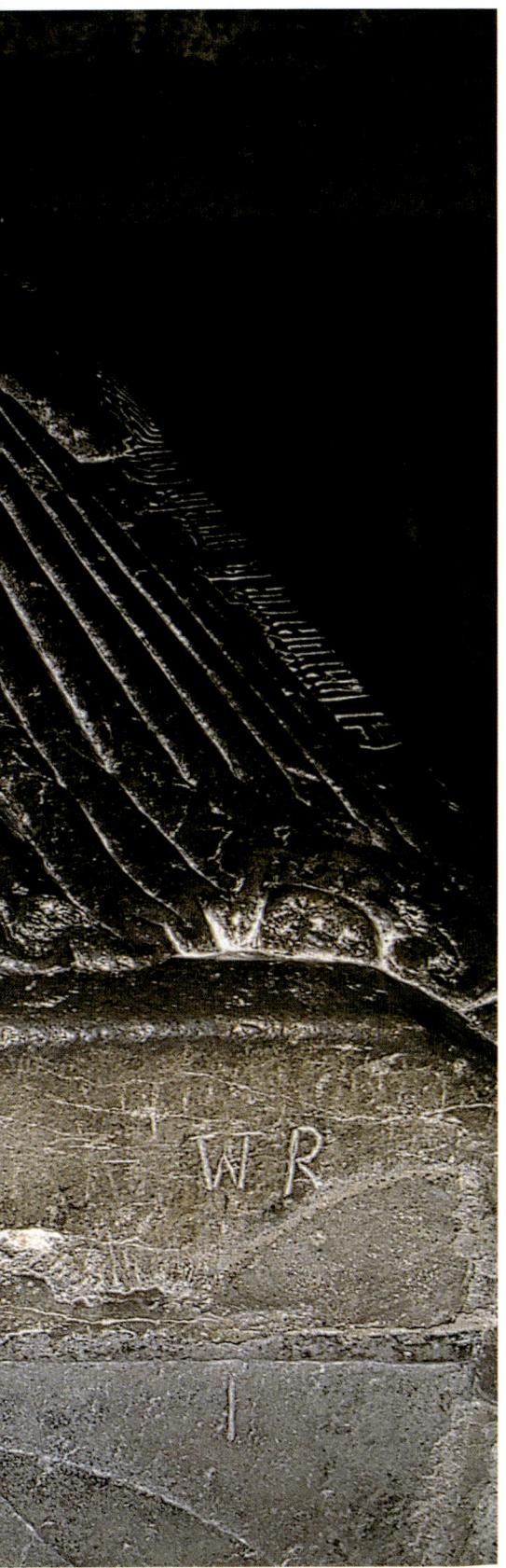

Effigies in St. Canice's Cathedral

Kilkenny

By the 15th century, two families descended from the Norman invaders had come to dominate most of Irish life. These were the Fitzgeralds ('Geraldines') and the Butlers. The Great Earl of Kildare, Gearóid Mór Fitzgerald, was viceroy and ruled Ireland almost like a king. The two most celebrated of his children were Gearóid Óg, who succeeded him in the earldom, and his daughter Margaret. In 1485, Margaret married the ambitious Piers Butler (known as *Piaras Rua*), who was an aspirant to the rival earldom of Ormond. The young couple were still in their teens and, with Geraldine assistance, Piaras Rua did in fact become 8th Earl of Ormond. He did not repay his in-laws with kindness, however, but did all in his power to destroy them. By skilfully taking the English side in disputes, he eventually succeeded.

Piaras became famous for his ambition and shrewdness, while Margaret (known as *Máiréad Ní Ghearóid*) was a commanding figure – tall, beautiful, and intensely loyal to her husband. Some of her contemporaries considered her extremely greedy, while others praised her 'hospitality and munificence'. Later folklore took the negative view, considering her to be hot-tempered and avaricious. It is said that she loved to accumulate land and other property, and often paid 'courtesy calls' to local landowners with this in mind. Such visits by her were much feared, since she had a craving appetite, and she tended to outstay her welcome and impoverish the unfortunate host. Piaras Rua died in 1539 and Máiréad three years later. They are buried together in St. Canice's Cathedral. The tomb is surmounted by fine effigies of them in high relief.

Blackstairs Mountains

Counties Wexford and Carlow

This long mountain range which forms the border between two counties is known from its appearance as *na Staighrí Dubha* ('the Black Stairs'). Notwithstanding this name, it is an area of great natural beauty, and boasts as its peak the aptly named Mount Leinster, which rises to a height of almost 2,625 feet (800 metres). In Irish, this peak is actually referred to as the *Suí* or 'Seat' of Leinster, because of the wonderful view to be had from there of much of the province.

It is said that a boy from that area once went to work in France. He was a handsome and dashing youth, and the daughter of the French king took a liking to him and brought him home to the palace to meet her people. The king naturally began to enquire about his family. The boy answered that he was of exalted lineage, his father being the king of Blackstairs with a seat on Mount Leinster. On further questioning, he revealed that, when sitting to table, his father always had a bearded guard with a halberd on each side of him. The same table-cloth was never used twice, and the food which was left over in the pot was always thrown out.

Duly impressed, the French king consented to the boy's marriage to his daughter. Later on, however, when he went to visit his royal counterpart on the Blackstairs, he found to his dismay that the mansion was but a tiny cottage near the top of the mountain. The 'king' sat to table with two billy-goats standing behind him. The 'table-cloth' was but a layer of straw which was wiped away after each meal, while a pig had its head in a pot eating the leftovers!

Domain of a fabled king.

Kilmore Quay
County Wexford

This picturesque fishing village is situated on the southern coast of Wexford. It takes its name from the Christian tradition, in Irish *An Chill Mhór* ('the large church-cell'), and it is home to the singing of a unique selection of Christmas carols. The words of these carols are in English, while the airs resemble singing styles in the Irish language. This in fact reflects the cultural history of the area, where a dialect of English was spoken from the Middle Ages but was heavily infuenced by the indigenous Irish language and its lore.

The singing of such carols was very rare in Ireland, and in County Wexford it dates to the 17th century and to the influence of two gentle clergymen working for impoverished communities. The earlier of the two, Fr Luke Wadding, belonged to an illustrious Catholic family of Wexford, who lost their lands in the Cromwellian confiscation. Having been ordained to the priesthood overseas in Salamanca, Fr Luke was appointed parish priest of New Ross in 1673 and became bishop of Ferns in 1683. In the following year he published in Ghent a collection of carols entitled *Smale Garland*. The second was Fr William Devereux, who became a priest in Salamanca a generation later. After his return to Ireland in 1728, Fr Devereux compiled a *Garland* of carols, which included some of Fr Luke's work and added much more. Many copies of this *Garland* circulated in manuscript, and the carols from it were sung in many churches in south Wexford. The custom survives in Kilmore Quay only. Alternate verses are sung by two groups of three men, and the full-throated and rhythmic performance, on a crisp Christmas morning, evokes a distinctive spiritual and aesthetic sense.

Loftus Hall
Fethard-on-Sea, County Wexford

In the extreme south of Leinster, on the Hook Peninsula, the Norman family of Redmond built a great mansion in the early 14th century. The house and surrounding lands were confiscated by the Cromwellians and given to the Loftus family in 1666, after which the name of the house was changed to 'Loftus Hall'. In the middle of the 18th century, the Honourable Charles Tottenham married Anne Loftus and went to live there. All went well until one stormy night, when a handsome stranger arrived on horseback seeking shelter from the weather. He was welcomed in and, having eaten, he joined in a game of cards, playing partner to the teenage daughter of the house. She was dealt a wonderful hand and was winning the game, but a card slipped from the table and she bent down to retrieve it. To her consternation, she saw that the stranger had, instead of a foot, a cloven hoof! She screamed, and he disappeared through the roof in a flash of fire. He reappeared periodically, much to the terror of the family, until the local priest, Fr Thomas Broaders, drove him away forever.

This is the oldest known Irish version of a cautionary legend against card-playing. It was based on the idea that heavy gambling was a trick of the devil to ensnare people, a point much stressed by parsons and priests. There were often rumours of hauntings in very old houses, and Loftus Hall being such, it was easy for the legend to become attached to that place. The venerable but rather sinister old building was demolished in 1871, and the new mansion erected on the site. Happily, no such hauntings affect the new building.

Pleasure in Pubs

Dublin

The ancients Celts of Europe held great drinking-parties at which tribal bonds were secured and treaties were made. The principal drink on such occasions was called *coirm*, a kind of ale made from a mash of barley or wheat fermented in water. The ancient Irish too drank this ale, while they listened to stories and music, and so popular were such parties in Ireland that the term *coirm* is now more often used to denote a music concert. According to tradition, indeed, the best feast was one which divided the night into three parts – one part for drinking, one for music, and one for pleasant sleep! As well as ale, the mediaeval Irish chieftains had a special taste for native mead and for Spanish wine, and a further ingredient for a pleasurable evening was, of course, good company.

The same spirit is to be found in the tavern or 'public-house' of more recent times. Apart from the more obvious drinkers seated near the 'bar', some more discreet clients retire to a cosy corner known as a 'snug', where there is a welcome only for those of sensible disposition and good conversation. The atmosphere in pubs is not always so restrained, however. Fine rollicking drinking-songs bear witness to exuberance and, although drunkenness is generally frowned upon, much humour attaches to the state of being 'merry'. The story is told of a man who took 'a little drop too much' and was repeatedly reprimanded by his parish priest on that account. One night, as the toper staggered home from the pub, he met his external conscience face to face. 'Drunk again, Pat!', remarked the priest meaningfully. 'So am I, Father!', answered Pat.

St. Patrick's Cathedral

Dublin

On the site of a little church dedicated to St. Patrick, the Norman conquerors of Dublin built a new and massive church in 1191. Raised to the status of cathedral in 1213, it has been extended and extensively repaired on several occasions. It is the largest church in Ireland, over 295 feet (90 metres) in length. A great tower, 147 feet (45 metres) high and out of line with the actual building, was added in the 14th century, and this was topped by a 100-foot (30-metre) granite spire four centuries later. From 1320 until the end of the 15th century the cathedral was the location for a University of Dublin, and with the Reformation it came into the possession of the Church of Ireland.

The most famous Dean of St. Patrick's was Jonathan Swift, clergyman, author, and fierce polemicist, who held that office from 1713 until his death in 1745. Readers and scholars all over the world have been fascinated by the writings of Swift, such as *The Battle of the Books*, *The Drapier Letters*, *A Modest Proposal*, and in particular *Gulliver's Travels*; but his keen satire and dramatic temperament also earned him great celebrity among the poor and unlettered of his day. He is a favourite figure in Irish folklore, in which he is represented as a witty eccentric who secretly sympathised with the cause of the oppressed people. Many humorous anecdotes tell of the cleverness of the Dean's apocryphal servant Jack, who continually outwits the indulgent but somewhat bemused master. Swift is buried in the grounds of the cathedral, beside Esther Johnson, the lady whom he called 'Stella' and with whom he enjoyed a close platonic friendship.

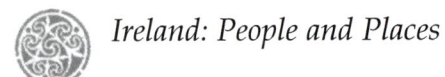

St. Patrick's Day Parade
Dublin

The great 5th-century missionary, St. Patrick, who became the patron of Ireland, seems to have died on March 17, for that has always been observed as his feastday. Down through the ages, he has been honoured in religious devotion, in scholarly research, and in popular legends, but much of the imagery today associated with him is not nearly so ancient. His connection with the shamrock seems to date only from the 16th century, with the custom of celebrating the feast with a glass of whiskey. This was called 'drowning the shamrock' for the little trefoil plant was used as an appetiser in drinking. Some wit then invented the fable that Patrick used the shamrock to explain the mystery of the Trinity to the pagan Irish.

More recent still is the holding of great parades through towns on St. Patrick's Day, led by brass and pipe bands. This originated in the 18th century in North America, where the British authorities held military parades on that day to encourage young Irishmen to join the army. After Independence, the U.S. Army recruited Irish immigrants in the same way, but the military trappings gradually diminished and the custom became so popular that it was adopted at home in Ireland. In the course of the 20th century, the St. Patrick's Day parades became ever more colourful and spread from the cities to smaller towns. They are accompanied by music, dance, and fancy dress, while various organisations, businesses, and community groups have their own promotional exhibits. Across the Atlantic a huge parade is held in New York, and smaller ones are now held in other parts of the world where the Irish have settled. The procession through the streets of Dublin is the most prestigious of all.

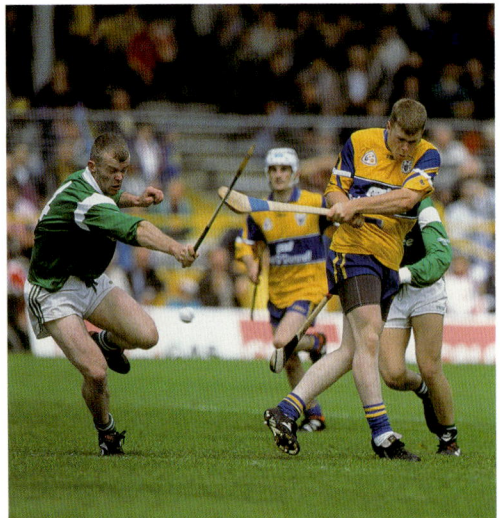

The origin of this most distinctive Irish sport is obscure, stretching back into prehistory. In the old epical stories, teams of champions played hurling-matches and there are descriptions of great individual prowess at the game. Various types of hurling (in Irish, *iomáint*) were practised long ago – in fields or on beaches, or indeed through a whole stretch of countryside – and there were differing methods of scoring. Since the foundation of the Gaelic Athletic Association in 1884, the rules of hurling have become standardised.

It is an amateur game, with two opposing teams, each with fifteen members playing on a rectangular field approximately 153 yards (140m) long and 87 yards (80m) wide. A team scores by driving the ball between the opposing uprights, tall poles set 20 feet (6.4m) apart. There is a crossbar, 7.8 feet (2.4m) high, between the uprights, and the ball passing under it amounts to a goal and over it to a point (value a third of a goal). Each player has a hurley (*camán*), fashioned from ash about 32 inches (92cm) long with a small knob on top for grip and widening at the bottom end into a curved flat base roughly 6.3 inches (16cm) across. The ball (*sliotar*) is round, 2.7 inches (7cm) in diameter, and consists of a leather covering on cork. The game lasts for an hour or, in cases of major contests, an hour and ten minutes. The ball may be struck at any height, and as a result hurling is the fastest field game in the world, being played with amazing courage and skill. The Final of the All-Ireland Senior Hurling Championship is the game's showpiece. It is held in early September each year at Croke Park, the national stadium of the Association, with about 70,000 cheering spectators in attendance.

Hurling at Croke Park

Dublin

Dublin Castle

Dublin

Built in the beginning of the 13th century, this castle was for seven hundred years the centre of English control in Ireland. It has been the headquarters of viceroys and lord lieutenants, and has often been the venue for State Councils and for Law Courts. It was besieged during the abortive rebellion of 'Silken' Thomas Fitzgerald, son of the Earl of Kildare, in 1534, and since then several plans were made by Irish revolutionaries to seize it. Such a plan was betrayed to the authorities in 1641 before it could be put into action; the seizure of the castle was to be the chief stratagem in Robert Emmet's intended rebellion in 1803; and in 1916 a plan to seize it was abandoned, even though – unknown to the rebels – it was poorly defended at the time. Celebrated Irishmen of many generations were imprisoned and executed there, and one of the most dramatic episodes in its history was the escape from captivity there of the young Donegal chieftain, Aodh Rua Ó Dónaill, in 1591.

The castle covers a large area, and most of the structures in their present form date from a massive programme of rebuilding in the 17th and 18th centuries. The Upper Castle Yard has two splendid gateways, and originally had several great drum towers, of which five survive in either full or fragmentary form. The modern State Apartments are in this part of the castle, and include St. Patrick's Hall, with elaborate paintings on the ceiling and with banners and armorial data on the walls. This Hall is the venue for major state occasions, and presidents of Ireland are inaugurated there. An archway leads to the Lower Castle Yard, where the great Record Tower and a fine Gothic chapel are situated.

The bastion that reflects history.

The Tomb of Strongbow

Christchurch, Dublin

When the deposed king of Leinster, Diarmaid Mac Murchadha, went to Britain to seek Norman aid to regain his dominion, one of the most eager adventurers he encountered was Richard de Clare, Earl of Pembroke, nicknamed 'Strongbow'. King Henry II had confiscated Strongbow's own estate in Wales, and the ambitious earl soon assented to Diarmaid's offer of his daughter in marriage and the succession to the Leinster kingship. In 1169, he sent an expedition to Ireland in support of Diarmaid, and in the following year he himself landed near Waterford with over 1,000 fighting men. He took that city after much slaughter, and married Diarmaid's daughter Aoife among the ruins.

After their combined forces took Dublin, Diarmaid unexpectedly died, leaving Strongbow to benefit from the second part of his contract, the kingship of Leinster. Fearing that Strongbow would set up a rival Norman kingdom, Henry II himself crossed to Ireland with a large army in 1171. Strongbow wisely submitted to his old king, but three years later he invaded Munster. Defeated by a strong Irish alliance near Thurles, he concentrated on consolidating his Leinster kingdom until his death in Dublin in 1176. It is said that the dead saints of Ireland conspired against him, and he even imagined that St. Brigid herself came from the otherworld to kill him! The earl of mixed fortunes was buried in Christchurch Cathedral, but his tomb was broken in a fall of the Cathedral's roof in 1562. In an attempt to repair the tomb some years later the effigy of another knight was mistakenly placed on it. In popular tradition, however, this figure of a knight in chain armour and the smaller figure beside it are still claimed to represent 'Strongbow and his son'.

The tomb with another man's image.

The Mansion House
Dublin

One of the finest residences in Dublin is the Mansion House, constructed between the years 1705 and 1710 for Sir Joshua Dawson, from whom the street where the house is situated gets its name. Dawson soon ran into financial difficulty, and in 1715 he sold the building to Dublin Corporation. Since then it has been the official residence of the Lord Mayor of the city. It originally had a red brick facade, but this has long been plastered and painted over. In the Victorian period, the original panels with figures were replaced by a balustrade, and other features were added such as a new portico and new windows. One of the most distinctive features of the house is the splendid stained glass window on the staircase, dating to the year 1900.

Attached to the house at the rear is the Round Room, designed and constructed hurriedly in 1821 for the visit of King George IV, who was honoured with a ball and banquet there. In a later generation the Mansion House served quite a different function, it being the venue for the assembly of the first Dáil Éireann, or independent Irish parliament. Following on the General Election of 1918, in which the Republicans gained a huge majority, 36 of their 73 elected representatives were arrested by the British authorities, and several more became fugitives, but the remaining 29 came together in the Mansion House on January 21, 1919, in order to declare Ireland a free nation. A president and various ministers were appointed by the Dáil, a programme of radical and egalitarian policies was adopted, and steps were taken to establish a new legal system. The British authorities quickly moved against the Dáil, and the War of Independence followed.

The house which, according to folklore, contains a secret vault of treasure.

St. Enda's Museum
Dublin

ádraic Pearse is the most celebrated of all Irish patriots. As well as a revolutionary leader, he was an accomplished author and educational philosopher. Born in Dublin in 1879 to an English father and an Irish mother, he joined the Gaelic League at the age of 16, began to write prose and poetry, and obtained a university degree in law. He became editor of the Gaelic League newspaper in 1903, and in 1908 he instituted a school for boys called *Scoil Éanna* (St. Enda's School) in the south Dublin suburb of Rathmines. Two years later, the school moved to a larger building with spacious grounds in Rathfarnham. Using the two languages, Irish and English, as media of instruction, the school was a model for an enlightened revolutionary Ireland, encouraging the boys to express and develop their own personality and abjure fear and tyranny.

Pearse joined the Irish Republican Brotherhood in 1913, and delivered a famous speech in 1915 at the burial of the old patriot Jeremiah O'Donovan Rossa. When the Easter Rising occurred in the following year, he was commander-in-chief of the rebel forces. After his surrender, he and his younger brother Willie were among those court-martialled and shot by the British Government. The poetry and short stories of Pearse give a clear insight into his character – these works instance a striking blend of mysticism and egalitarianism in which he glorifies the socially weak, the ignored and the marginalised ('the people that sorrow'). The building in which he conducted his school in Rathfarnham is now a museum and cultural centre dedicated to his ideals, and to the memory of him and his comrades.

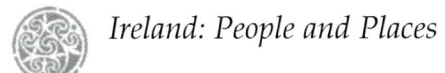

The Guinness Brewery
Dublin

There were many small breweries in 18th-century Ireland. One such was established in Leixlip, County Kildare, by Arthur Guinness in the year 1756. Guinness was the son of a land-agent, and he proved an able businessman, being owner of a successful flourmill also. His brewery thrived, and in 1759 he decided to relocate it to Dublin, purchasing the site of a small disused premises at St. James' Gate. Before long, Guinness' brewery was outstripping all its rivals in that city, and had even begun to export on a large scale to Britain.

Ale and beer were the principal products, but after 1790 – under the direction of Guinness' son, also named Arthur – the brewery began to specialise in the drink called 'porter'. This in time developed into 'stout', the strong dark beer with creamy froth on top, to which so many people of different classes and nationalities have become enamoured. This is the drink with which the Guinness name is associated all over the world today, although in actual fact that family retain only a tiny share in the company. The brewery once housed the largest tun in the world, made of stainless steel and measuring over 62 feet (19 metres) in length and almost 30 feet (9 metres) in width, and capable of fermenting 7,800 bulk barrels of stout at one brewing. Over a thousand people are employed on the site, the daily output being no less than four million pints. The complex of buildings at the Guinness brewery is vast, and it even contains a museum and cultural centre modelled from the former hop store. The company is also noted for its catching advertisements, with slogans such as 'Guinness is good for you!' and 'My goodness, my Guinness!'.

River Boyne

(various counties)

Rising at Clonkeen in north County Kildare, this great river flows in a semi-circle through a small piece of County Offaly and into the plain of Meath, before heading eastwards for a long way until it meets the Irish Sea at Drogheda. It was anciently said to have been the abode of a goddess who gave sustenance and wisdom to the whole surrounding countryside. This goddess was called *Bóinn*, an archaic name which meant 'she who is cow-like and illuminating'. The river itself was often regarded as being synonymous with the goddess, and so its whole course was anciently described as being a sacred conduit of wisdom. One who drank water from this river in the month of June, it was said, gained the gift of poetry, for the sun impregnated the water with wisdom at this time.

One tradition was that the well at the source of the Boyne was surrounded by nine hazel-trees, the nuts of which were full of wisdom. When these nuts dropped into the water and floated down the Boyne, they were consumed by the fish there. It was said that one particular salmon in the river was full of wisdom, and that whoever caught and ate that salmon would acquire it all. An old seer fished for it for many years and finally caught it, and he asked the boy-champion Fionn Mac Cumhaill to cook it for him on a spit. Fionn did so, but when he noticed a blister rising on the salmon he unwittingly put his thumb to it. The thumb was burnt, and he put the thumb into his mouth to ease the pain. Immediately all the knowledge came to Fionn, and from that day on he was a great poet and prophet.

Lia Fáil Stone
County Meath

The Hill of Tara was the most important sacred centre of ancient Ireland, and was the seat of power of the high-kings of the country for several centuries. It abounds in ancient monuments, including raths, tumuli, embankments, and enclosures. This granite standing-stone was formerly situated on the 'Mound of the Hostages', a small prehistoric passage-grave at Tara where kings were inaugurated. It was, however, in recent centuries transferred to another mound about 130 yards (120 metres) to the south, where it now stands in an equally prominent position.

The Lia Fáil is a carved round-topped monolith, reaching to a height of 5.2 feet (1.6 metres) overground. Its name means 'the stone of Fál', and this archaic word *fál* has been interpreted in many ways – the most probable sense was 'prosperity'. It was clearly the most important ritual stone in the country, and the mythologists claimed that it had been brought to Ireland by the divine race called Tuatha Dé Danann. It is, at any rate, clear that the stone was a phallic symbol, and that it represented the fertility of good kingship. In popular tradition, it was known as *Bod Fhearghusa* ('the phallus of Fearghus'), and it is significant that the name *Fearghus* meant literally 'male vigour' and was one of the designations of the ancestor-deity. One old account gives a dramatic description of the selection of a king at Tara. The aspirant was put in a chariot drawn by two unbroken stallions, and the horses then raced towards the Lia Fáil. When the chariot's axle touched it, the Lia Fáil cried out to announce the coming of the true king.

The ancient cultic stone of prosperity at Tara, survivor from a forgotten world.

ituated on the river Shannon, Athlone (in Irish, *Baile Átha Luain*) has always been the main artery for traffic between the provinces of Leinster and Connacht. At the end of the best-known epic of early Ireland, a defeated Connacht army retreats over the bridge of Athlone led by the warrior-queen Meadhbh. An elderly warrior in her troop remarks that 'a herd of horses led by a mare never fared well!'. Down through the centuries, various bridges were constructed at this site, as well as various fortresses and castles to protect them. The present castle, curtain-walls, and drum-shaped towers, date from the 13th century.

Athlone was a Jacobite stronghold during the 'War of the Two Kings', and so the Williamite army under General Ginkel advanced to attack it in June of 1691. The Jacobite commander was Marechal St. Ruth, a French officer who had recently arrived in Ireland, and against better advice he decided to hold the town. The Williamites were held at bay by a small force of defenders, who succeeded in destroying the arches of the bridge before swimming to safety on the western bank. That western part of Athlone was then heavily bombarded for seven days by the Williamite army, in preparation for a full frontal assault. Finally the attackers set planks on the broken arches and prepared to cross. A Jacobite dragoon sergeant called Custume volunteered to cut the planks and, with ten men armed with axes and saws, swam into the river. They were cut to pieces by the enemy fire, but their work was completed by eleven others, of whom only two survived. The Williamites eventually took the town by storm, but the courage of the gallant Sergeant Custume and his men was admired by all.

Athlone
County Westmeath

Ardee
County Louth

This town takes its name from a local branch of a far-flung ancient tribe known as the Fir Deadhadh, or 'men of campaigning'. The river-ford (*áth*) there was thus known as Áth Fhear Deadhadh. In time this toponymic was understood to refer to a special individual champion, called Fear Deadh or Fear Dia, and hence it was reformulated as Áth Fhir Dia, from which the English version comes. Early mediaeval writers speculated that the name might have meant 'man of the goddess' or 'divine man', and this heightened his profile so that he was easily adopted into the epic of the Cattle-Raid of Cooley, which was being rapidly developed by storytellers at the time.

Once accepted into the cast of characters for the epic, Fear Dia came to be portrayed as a young warrior, friend, and ultimately rival of the super-hero Cú Chulainn. The two young men had been comrades in arms, but they found themselves on opposite sides when Queen Meadhbh of Connacht launched her attack on Ulster so as to seize the great bull of Cooley. Cú Chulainn singlehandedly kept Meadhbh's army at bay, and she soon realised that nobody could oppose him except Fear Dia. She offered Fear Dia all kinds of rewards to take the field against his friend, but he refused until she slyly accused him of being afraid of Cú Chulainn. The epic goes on to describe in detail the tragic combat between the two friends on the river-ford at Ardee. After three days of fighting, Cú Chulainn used the one trick that his friend did not know – he threw a barbed javelin from between his toes into the stomach of his friend, fatally wounding him. Fear Dia died in his arms.

ULSTER

Christmas mummers in County Tyrone – a hilarious dash of colour.

Mountsandel

County Derry

This is the earliest known place to be inhabited in all of Ireland. Known in Irish as Dún Dá Bheann ('the fortress of two peaks'), it is situated about a mile and a quarter (2 kilometres) south of Coleraine, on the east bank of the river Bann. People were here more than 8,000 years ago, at one site on a ridge-top above the flat river valley, and at another on a narrow ledge over the river itself. This community was not, however, an isolated one, for there are several indications of contact with other groups further south in the country – groups who have left no remains or, if they did, whose remains have not been found. The people at Mountsandel lived in small circular huts, about 20 feet (6 metres) in diameter, with saplings and sods or hides for walls and with a hearth in the centre of each hut.

We know little about these Mesolithic inhabitants, what they looked like, what languages they spoke, what religious beliefs they had. Their ancestors had come into the country, possibly by a thin land-bridge which may still have existed, but more likely by travelling in small boats. Excavations at Mountsandel have shown that they hunted and ate wild pig, hare and birds, that they fished for salmon and eel, and that they supplemented their diet with hazel-nuts and wild crab-apples. For cutting they used thin blades about an inch and a half (4 centimetres) long called microliths, which were chipped from flint and chert; and they also had some axes of ground flint. Their lifestyle was simple and mundane by comparison with the ancient peoples of Ireland as imagined by the mythologists, but all indications are that they were already in the process of developing a distinctive Irish culture.

The oldest remains of human habitation in Ireland bear their silent witness.

It was traditional in Ireland, since the Middle Ages at least, to hold special markets for specific types of animals. There were not only fairs for cattle and horses, but also special pig-fairs, goat-fairs, and even dog-fairs. Sometimes, a particular animal would be kept on a raised platform, as a symbol of the fair for its duration. This practice was followed with a white horse in Cappawhite, County Tipperary. A billy-goat was similarly displayed at the fair of Mullinavat, County Kilkenny; and such a display at the celebrated 'puck-fair' in Killorglin, County Kerry, continues as a major festival attraction in early August each year. During an old three-day ram-fair in Greencastle, County Down, a ram was likewise exhibited.

There is a fine example, with plenty of appropriate atmosphere, of a fair devoted to sheep at Draperstown. This was established in 1792, when the town was still known by its old name of *Baile na Croise* ('the town of the cross'). Not only is the sheep the most numerous domesticated animal in Ireland, but it is also one of the oldest. Mediaeval scholars claimed, indeed, that a small herd was brought in a boat by the fantastic lady Cessair, reputedly the leader of the first group of people to settle in the country. One old story tells of how the hero Fionn Mac Cumhaill and his companions were overcome by a vigorous ram, and a wise old man explained to them that the ram symbolised the energy of the whole world. In ordinary folk belief, the sheep was considered a lucky animal, and if one looked through the shoulder-blade of a dead sheep one might see into the future.

Sheep-fair, Draperstown
County Derry

Tory Island
County Donegal

Like other European peoples, the ancient Celts had a myth of a great battle between two sets of deities at the beginning of the world. In Ireland, the myth was developed in such a way as to locate that battle at some great imagined pillar in the sea. One such place lies off the north-west coast of Donegal, overlooking the wild Atlantic. It is called *Oileán Toraí*, in earlier form *Tor-Inis*, the import of both names being 'towery island'. Because of its remoteness and its evocative pinnacled appearance, from the mainland the whole island could easily be imagined as a sort of tower where the waters meet with the skies.

The island has been inhabited since antiquity. Tradition claims that it was the residence of Balar, king of the destructive deities called Fomhoire who lived in the watery regions and who fought against the bright deities called Tuatha Dé Danann. Balar had a destructive eye in his forehead, which destroyed all on which he looked, burning up landscapes and reducing men and beasts to ashes. Hearing a prophecy that he would be slain by his own grandchild, he kept his only daughter locked in a tower on the island so that no man could gain access to her. She did meet a young man, however, and when Balar realised that she was pregnant he ordered that the baby be killed immediately upon its birth. The baby was a beautiful boy, and the soldiers of Balar took pity on him and allowed him to be spirited away to the mainland, where he grew up to be the divine champion Lugh, leader of the Tuatha Dé Danann. In the great primordial battle, Lugh confronted his tyrant grandfather, pierced the terrible eye, and slew him. On the more level end of the island, a lighthouse stands today.

Killybegs Harbour
County Donegal

Ireland being an island, fish is an important part of the staple diet of the people. In times of scarcity and even famine, coastal dwellers have often been preserved by the abundant harvest of the sea. According to an old Irish saying, 'though every profession may falter, fishing will prosper'. Given the unpredictability of the sea, however, misfortune and tragedy are never far away from the life of the Irish fisherman, especially along the wild Atlantic coast. In folklore, the sea is compared to a great and powerful being which must have its will. A person being saved from drowning was a cause for joy and celebration, but the folk were wont to grow more cautious thereafter, as the vengeful sea might demand a substitute victim. There are special beliefs, too, concerning the catch. If a fox is seen by fishermen when going down to their boats, they take this as a sign that no fish are to be had that day. The fox, with its russet coat, is too much a symbol of the land and is thus inappropriate to the watery surroundings. Neither the fox nor a red-haired woman should be mentioned in a fishing-boat, nor should – for some reason – a priest be spoken of. The blessing of a priest at the start of the fishing season is, however, highly valued.

In manifold ways of its own, the sea compensates, and few sights are more satisfying than that of the fishing fleet laden with silver herrings returning at evening under a slanting sun. Killybegs (*Na Cealla Beaga* – 'the small churches') is one of the leading fishing-ports in contemporary Ireland. Its fishermen are to the fore in efforts to protect this age-old Irish industry in the face of quotas and falling fish-stock.

Tullaghogue
County Tyrone

The longest dynastic rule in Ireland began in the 5th century AD, when a tribe called Connachta occupied Tara in County Meath. Their great king was called Niall, and from him the leading family of the tribe took the name *Uí Néill* ('descendants of Niall'). In the singular this is *Ó Néill*, and when patronymics developed into surnames in the Middle Ages this became the most prestigious surname in Ireland. The great Uí Néill family claimed the High-Kingship of Ireland, and most of the country was under their sway for centuries. They divided early into two leading branches – the northern Uí Néill in Ulster and the southern Uí Néill in the plain of Meath. For many centuries, indeed, these two branches alternated the High-Kingship between them by common agreement.

Eventually, other septs succeeded in wresting the High-Kingship from them in the 11th century, and within a few generations Ireland came to be ruled by the Anglo-Norman kings from London. In these circumstances, the northern Uí Néill maintained all of their family pride and the hope of one day regaining their premier place in Irish life. Their inauguration site was at *Tulach Óg* ('hillock of the young warriors'), two-and-half miles (4 kilometres) south of Cookstown in County Tyrone. Within the ring-fort there, the Ó Néill chieftain was proclaimed leader of his people while sitting on a stone chair. The last of the great chieftains of this family was Aodh Ó Néill, Earl of Dungannon, leader of the Irish in the 'Nine Years War' against the Elizabethan armies. He died in Italy in 1616, at the age of 76. In his cups, the old leader would sometimes remark: 'There will be a fine sunny day in Ireland yet!'

A chain of hills curves around the great city of Belfast. Overlooking the city to the north, and rising to a height of 1,190 feet (363 metres), is the prominence called in Irish *Binn Uamha* ('peak of the cave') and in English 'Cave Hill'. There are in fact no fewer than three caves in the massive cliff-face on the east of the hill. The place once had another name also, being known as *Binn Mhadagáin*, the peak of a certain Madagán, a king of Ulster who died there in 856 AD. As one approaches from Belfast, the hill's outline looks strikingly like a reclining human body, with brow, nose, lips, and chin in clear profile against the sky.

There is a strong univallate ring-fort on the very edge of the cliff, above the caves. This is called MacArt's Fort, after the chieftain Brian Mac Airt Ó Néill, who was slain by the Lord Deputy Mountjoy during the Elizabethan Wars in 1601. It was here, in the year 1795, that Theobald Wolfe Tone and his friends convened in order to pledge themselves never to desist in their struggle for Irish independence. Tone, a Protestant from Dublin, was visiting his fellow revolutionaries in the northern city. Their organisation was called the United Irishmen, and most of the Belfast leaders were Presbyterians by religion. The basic aim of the movement was to bring all the Irish people together, and they hoped to get assistance from revolutionary France to establish a republic. Their hopes ended in an orgy of government repression in 1798, however, and most of the leaders were rounded up and put to death. Tone himself died in prison – apparently by his own hand – while awaiting execution.

Cave Hill
County Antrim

Orange Parade
County Down

The Dutch leader William of Orange (1650-1702) was married to the daughter of James II of England, and when his father-in-law was deposed in 1689 he was enthroned as William III. The subsequent war between James and William was fought in Ireland, with the crucial victory being gained by William in the Battle of the Boyne, fought near Oldbridge in County Meath on July 1 of the year 1690 (according to the revised calendar July 11). There are many popular traditions about this battle – James is claimed to have behaved like a coward and fled the battlefield, while William was courageous and was undaunted by wounds and by ill-health. One officer from the Jacobite army is said to have cried out to the Williamites at the end of the battle, 'Exchange leaders, and we will fight you again!'

This victory of William over James determined the political system which prevailed in Ireland through the succeeding century – the Protestant ascendancy over Catholics and Presbyterians. Within a few generations, however, a new radical movement, the United Irishmen, sought to unite members of all three religions under a common banner of equality and Irish independence from Britain. In reaction to this, the Orange Order was founded in 1795, with the memory of William as the inspiring force. An imaginative painting of the king astride a fine white charger, done by Benjamin West in 1771, provided the imagery, and the Orange Lily became the emblem. 'King Billy' was portrayed as the champion of all Protestant denominations and the implacable enemy of 'Popery' and of republicanism. The great celebration of this sentiment remains the Twelfth of July, with its large and trenchant parades and strong expressions of loyalty to Britain.

Dundrum Bay
County Down

The ancient name of this wide and picturesque bay was the *Loch* or 'lake' of *Rudhraighe*, this being the designation of the tribe from whom most of the storied Ulster heroes were sprung. In fact, the corpus of epical tales concerning these heroes is known in Irish as *Rudhraigheacht*. In the bay was one of the four great waves of Ireland, and on the death of a king this wave was heard to cry out its lamentation.

One of the greatest of the heroes was Fearghus Mac Léide, described by the mythologists as a very early king of Ulster. It is said that, on one occasion when he was at the coast, Fearghus encountered a group of sea-sprites, who granted him three wishes – namely, the power to swim under seas, pools, and lakes. There was, however, one exception, for they stipulated that he must never swim in Loch Rudhraighe. Time passed, and the bravery of Fearghus got the upper hand of his caution, so he did go to swim in that bay. While under the water, he encountered a dreadful monster, which alternately inflated and contracted itself. Fearghus fled to the shore, and he was so terror-stricken that his mouth was turned to the back of his head. Such a blemish would disqualify him from the kingship, so his advisers conspired to hide it from the public. The plan succeeded for seven years, but finally a servant noticed the blemish, and Fearghus – consumed with shame – returned to the bay to fight the monster. After a fearsome tussle, which lasted a whole day and night, he slew the monster, but as soon as he swam ashore he collapsed and died from exhaustion. For a whole month, the bay remained red from the bloodshed.

Scene of the oldest Irish story of 'the little people',
fairy dwellers on the land and sea.

Loughbrickland
County Down

On either side of the main road from Dublin to Belfast, just over 9 miles (15 kilometres) north of Newry, lie the little lake known as Loughbrickland and the village of the same name. In the original Irish the toponymic is *Loch Bricreann*, meaning 'the lake of Bricriu'. Who this Bricriu ('little speckled fellow') was in reality we do not know, but the name was sufficiently evocative for an early Irish writer to imagine him as a troublesome fellow who wrought havoc among the Ulster heroes with his malicious tricks. He is described as a satirist, probably because a type of false praise mixed with blame was referred to as 'speckled praise'.

Bricriu is said to have been notoriously two-faced and wily, and he once boasted that 'a whisper is more valuable to me than a roar to another person'. The principal story concerning him tells of how he invited all the Ulster nobles to a feast in his dwelling. It was customary for the greatest warrior at a feast to receive a special joint of meat called 'the champion's portion', and Bricriu variously promised this to the three leading heroes. To add to the confusion, he told each of their wives that the first of the women to enter the feast would be considered the most noble. The women were first to fight, and the three husbands could be restrained from attacking each other only by the king, Conchobhar, arranging an elaborate series of tests for them. At these tests, Cú Chulainn proved to be the bravest and best, and to him the champion's portion was awarded. According to the 'Cattle-Raid of Cooley', Bricriu was trampled and slain by the two great bulls who fought each other at the end of that epic.

The beautiful lake which, it is said, once belonged to a satirist with a poisoned tongue.

The border area straddling south Ulster and north Leinster was, in the 18th and early 19th centuries, one of the leading parts of Ireland in terms of Gaelic scholarship. Several celebrated poets lived there – including Séamas Mac Cuarta, Art Mac Cumhaigh, and Peadar Ó Doirnín. Lingering traditions of these, and anecdotes concerning them, portrayed the archetypal poet as an independent soul, somewhat bohemian in his life style, a quasi-magician who used his satiric powers to censor greed and pomposity in society. A young person growing up in that countryside in succeeding generations was heir to lore of this type which magnified the role of the poet.

Such a young man was Patrick Kavanagh (1905-1967), a native of Inniskeen, who knew little Irish but was inspired by the local idea that poets had special powers. His own poetry also was rooted in his native area, but differed substantially from that of his Gaelic predecessors in that it contained none of the old learned allusions but instead focused on spontaneous impressions gleaned from the landscape and from the social life of his own time. Looking into an ordinary field, for instance, he could say: 'This is the source from which all cultures rise, and all religions; there is the pool in which the poet dips, and the musician'. He claimed that his inspiration was 'elemental', but his great gift of seizing the aesthetic depth of the ordinary moment would make him feel at home with other poets of any epoch. In 1939, he went to live in Dublin, and pondered on the image which he wished to have in the eyes of the city-dwellers. Echoing the poet-lore of his native countryside, he described himself as 'dangerous', 'eccentric', 'slothful', 'a nice man', and 'a lone one'.

The Kavanagh Museum

Inniskeen, County Monaghan

Mummers

(various counties)

D rama as a developed art-form was not a feature of Gaelic Ireland, although there was a strong dramatic element to public storytelling, to the recitation of poetry, and to the various musical and comical performances at the courts of chieftains. There was also a rich celebration of seasonal festivals, particularly at the four cardinal points of the Celtic calendar – the beginnings of spring, summer, autumn, and winter. It was customary for groups of people to congregate and to boisterously celebrate such festivals, and this often involved the wearing of disguise and rather elaborate miming.

Staged drama as such was first introduced into Dublin by the English settlers in the 14th century, and it soon spread into other towns. There is evidence that, by the beginning of the 17th century, folk plays of the type known in England were spreading from the towns into the surrounding countryside. The word 'mummery', meaning 'masked performance', itself came from England, being based on the mediaeval French *mommerie*. These folk-plays soon mixed with the age-old native seasonal festivities, and so the tradition of mumming became well established in large parts of Ireland – particularly in the provinces of Ulster and Leinster. A performance entails rhetorical and humorous speeches, delivered by actors disguised as religious characters such as St. George, St. Patrick, and the devil; mediaeval military characters such as the Grand Signior and the Grand Turk; and more recognisable figures such as Oliver Cromwell, Napoleon, the Czar of Russia, and Daniel O'Connell. The speeches are accompanied by combative gestures and feigned hand-to-hand fighting. The custom is usually practised during the fortnight preceding Christmas, and colourful mumming troupes can still be encountered in Fermanagh, west Tyrone, mid-Antrim, Sligo, north Dublin, and south Wexford.

Bowling
County Armagh

The Irish people have a long and varied tradition of field-sports. The native game of hurling, noted for its antiquity as well as for its skill, may well have been the ultimate source of similar games of stick and ball once played in England, from which hockey is sprung. On the other hand, several games came into Ireland from abroad – particularly the several variants of football. A mediaeval Irish adaptation of such a folk game in Britain gave rise to what is now known as Gaelic football, whereas rugby and soccer have been introduced in more recent times and also have large followings in Ireland.

Another open-air sport which was adopted from Britain was played with a small ball of crude iron. This had wide popularity in 19th-century Ireland, but more recently has survived principally in two counties separated from each other by a long distance, Cork (where it is called 'bowling') and Armagh (where it is called 'bullet throwing'). Two players contend in throwing the little round ball, which is 3 inches (7.62 centimetres) in diameter and weighs 28 ounces (almost 800 grams). The course is usually along a road, with look-outs to prevent any accident with oncoming traffic; and a set distance is arranged, usually about 3 miles (5 kilometres). The player who can cover that distance with the least amount of throws is the winner. When a contest is arranged between two champions, stakes are arranged and a considerable amount of wagers are laid on each side. The method of throwing is the most effective for such a projectile, underhand and jerking upwards to shoulder-height before releasing it, and the drama of these contests enlivens many a rural Sunday afternoon.

MUNSTER

Praying at the holy well in County Clare.

The Burren
County Clare

This is a place which, hundreds of millions of years ago, grew out of sediments of the sea compressed into limestone. Then the sea level sank, but the waters returned once more, forming strata of shale, and finally great movements of the earth's crust thrust the whole region above the water again to form a plateau. The face of this plateau was later marked and torn by glacials in the Ice Age, the hills being given their present shape and the rocks fissured still further. All of this left a landscape of marked contrast and great beauty – a dry, barren, and white place, with a multitude of underground streams and springs. In the darkness underneath, too, there are vast caves, the most celebrated being that underneath *Aill Bhuí* ('yellow cliff'), which is situated just south of Ballyvaughan.

Covering the whole of north-west Clare, the region derives its name aptly from the Irish *Boireann*, meaning 'rocky country'. Here the forces of nature have combined to give unique results. The clefted rocks and trapped soil, fed by the abundant water welling up into temporary ponds, have met with the mild and moist air blowing in from the Atlantic Ocean along the coast from Black Head in the north to the massive cliffs of Moher in the south. So the Burren is host to an extraordinary mixture of flora and fauna. Plants and wild flowers of Arctic, Alpine, and Mediterranean varieties abound, and there are no fewer than twenty-eight species of butterfly, as well as many types of birds and small animals. People came early to the Burren, as is evidenced by its many archaeological remains, and countless generations have eked out an existence from the sparse but fruitful soil.

A great white world of stone.

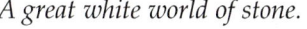

Kincora
Killaloe, County Clare

Towards the end of the 10th century, a new sept rose to power in Munster. This was the Dál gCais, from the area west of the bend in the river Shannon, and its leader was Mathghamhain. Having defeated the Vikings of Limerick in bloody campaigns, Mathghamhain took the kingship of the province in 968, but eight years later he was slain by Irish rivals and his younger brother Brian Boru took over. In his youth, Brian had been a brilliant guerrilla leader, and now he proved himself an even more accomplished ruler than his brother. Through a mixture of diplomacy and military action, he managed to wrest the High-Kingship of Ireland from the reigning sovereign in 1002. He was prudent as well as ambitious, and had a great gift for organisation. A patron of learning and monasteries, he signed himself 'Emperor of the Irish' in the Book of Armagh. In his old age he scored his greatest victory, against a strong Viking army at the battle of Clontarf near Dublin. Towards the end of the battle, however, he was surprised and slain by a fleeing Viking warrior.

Brian had his palace at Kincora, from the Irish *Ceann Cora* ('head of the weir'), on the hill to the west of the bridge at Killaloe. That picturesque town itself developed from the little monastery called Cill Dalua ('church of holy Lua'), situated just south of the bridge. Lua was a saint of the 7th century, and Brian Boru – wishing to perpetuate the memory of that holy man – had a church built and dedicated to him on the site of his monastery. In the 12th century, this was replaced by the fine cathedral of Killaloe which still stands today.

Spanish Point
County Clare

In July of the year 1588 a great Spanish fleet, called the Armada, set sail from La Coruña. It comprised 65 galleons, 25 store-ships, and 30 smaller vessels, and carried about 30,000 men. The plan was to sail to Flanders, and to support the crossing from there of an even larger Spanish army to invade England. They were scattered by the English fleet in the Channel, however, and had to escape into the North Sea. They eventually rounded Scotland and headed into the Atlantic, where terrible misfortunes awaited them. Many of the ships were wrecked off the west coast of Ireland, and thousands of soldiers and sailors were drowned.

One of their worst disasters occurred on the coast of Clare, in the area around the headland which as a result is known as *Rinn na Spáinneach* or Spanish Point. There, in September 1588, the *San Marcos*, with 409 men aboard, was wrecked, only four of the crew surviving. The *San Esteban* was wrecked a few miles further south, with sixty survivors, and all were seized by the high sheriff of Clare, Baothghalach Mac Fhlannchadha (Boethius McClancy). He belonged to a long line of Gaelic nobles and scholars, but had gone into the service of Elizabeth and now wasted no time in hanging all the Spanish prisoners. This callous act shocked combatants on all sides, and it was long remembered. There was a tradition that the widows of the hanged men met every seventh year on the altar steps of a church in Spain to place a curse on Boethius McClancy. The high sheriff died in 1598, and it was said that he often reappeared as a fiery ghost with his legs thin from suffering in the afterlife.

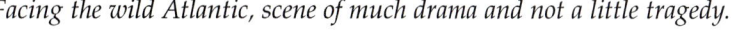

Facing the wild Atlantic, scene of much drama and not a little tragedy.

Scattery Island
County Clare

Midway across the broad mouth of the river Shannon lies an island known in Irish as *Inis Cathaigh* ('Isle of the Battler') and in English from a Viking corruption of that name as 'Scattery'. In area the island is about 72 hectares (almost 180 acres, 72,000 square metres). Some families lived there until recent times and, though there are still some houses, sheep and cattle are now the only full-time inhabitants. The island is celebrated for the monastery founded there in the early 6th century by a saint called Seanán. This seems to have been a nickname, for it means 'old man', and most of our information concerning the saint is obscure. It is said that he belonged to a sept of west Clare, and that he banished a great reptilic monster from Scattery before he settled there.

The king who ruled the Limerick side of the river claimed the island, and he sent his wizard to contend with Seanán, but to no avail. Later, a holy lady called Canair walked across the waters of the Shannon to the island and insisted that Seanán allow a convent to be founded there in tandem with his monastery. After some argument, he consented to this and the island became so celebrated for its sanctity that Seanán was numbered among the five leading monks of Ireland.

As well as some remains of the original monastery, there are ruins of five later mediaeval churches on Scattery, and a well-preserved round tower over 115 feet (35 metres) in height. Because of its situation, in the broad estuary facing the Atlantic Ocean, and of its miraculous associations, some curious beliefs attached to the place. New boats were sailed around Scattery on the starboard side, and pebbles from the island were believed to protect sailors from drowning.

Knockfeerina

County Limerick

Standing with a view over the wide and rich plain of County Limerick, just east of the town of Ballingarry, is a small peaked mountain 950 feet (290 metres) high. Its original name was taken from the old designation of the plain, *Frithghrinn*, but for many centuries now that name *Cnoc Frithghrinne* has been corrupted into *Cnoc Fírinne*, with the meaning 'hill of truth'. All indications are that it was a sacred site in pre-Christian Ireland, and it has long been regarded as an otherworldly place. Weather prognostications are taken by observing the appearance of the hill – mist or cloud-cap portending rain, a clear view portending good weather.

The hill was one of the favourite residences of the ancient god of the dead, Donn, and many stories tell of his appearance in the neighbourhood as a ghostly rider on a white horse, sometimes flying through the air in thunderous weather. He is said to be a splendid horseman, and is known to have appeared to blacksmiths on occasion to have his mount shod. Although somewhat mysterious, Donn is not regarded as hostile, being often represented as a helper and a good adviser to those in distress. Until recent times, many people believed that Donn was real, and there was even a lingering feeling that after death one spent some time in the hill with him before moving on to the Christian afterlife. It is also claimed that he is king of the Munster fairies and that he and his troupe fight a battle each May and November against the Connacht fairies led by Fionnbharra. This is in reality a late echo of the seasonal contests of ancient myth between a bright figure called Fionn (representing summer) and a dark figure called Donn (representing winter).

Ballyneety

Pallasgreen, County Limerick

During the siege of Limerick in 1690, King William decided to bring a huge consignment of cannon from England in order to batter down the walls of that city. This 'siege train' was on its way from Dublin, and the defenders in Limerick knew that if it arrived all would be lost. The dashing cavalry officer Patrick Sarsfield was determined to prevent this and, at the dead of night, he assembled a large company of horsemen in the city and had the feet of their mounts muffled with cloths so that the hoof-beats could not be heard by the vigilant enemy outside the walls.

They left the city unnoticed by the northern gate, and rode north for a long distance before crossing the Shannon at Killaloe. Their guide was the outlaw leader Dónall Ó hÓgáin, and he brought them south through the Slievefelim mountains towards Ballyneety on the border between the counties of Limerick and Tipperary, where the siege train had stopped for the night. It is said that one of their horses cast a shoe, and that Sarsfield told its rider to walk the horse and wait for the other cavalrymen to return. This rider soon met a woman, the wife of an English soldier, who conversed with him and let out the secret that the password for the siege-train was Sarsfield's own name. Thereupon the rider rushed after the horsemen with this news. Using the password, Sarsfield gained entry to the camp and then shouted out: 'Sarsfield is the word and Sarsfield is the man!' His riders quickly piled all the wagons together, and blew up the lot in a tremendous explosion. William, outside the walls of Limerick, saw the night-sky light up to the south and immediately knew what had happened.

The Collegiate Church
Kilmallock, County Limerick

A holy man settled here in the 7th century, giving his name to the place, *Cill Mocheallóg* (meaning 'the church of the beloved Ceallóg'). The town as such was, however, the creation of the Normans. Despite its tempestuous history, including being sacked during the Elizabethan and Cromwellian Wars, so many of its splendid old buildings have survived that Kilmallock has been colourfully termed 'the Baalbek of Ireland'. One can observe there not only the remains of Ceallóg's little church, but also a castle, a substantial stretch of the town walls as well as one of the mediaeval town gates, some old town houses, and the ruins of two large mediaeval churches.

One of these is the Collegiate Church of Saints Peter and Paul, 'the great church of Kilmallock', which dates to the 13th century. The transept is original, but most of the other features date from 1420, when the structure was enlarged. The chancel measures about 50 by 25 feet (15 by 8 metres), the nave is about 80 by 65 feet (24 by 20 metres), and incorporated within the building are the remains of a pre-Norman round tower. The building functioned as a kind of cathedral from the 15th century onwards, and in 1541 the entire college of canons there gave their allegiance to the Reformation. It was the scene in 1573 of the submission of the famous rebel, James Fitzmaurice Fitzgerald, to Sir John Perrott; and seventeen years later of the attempt by the English to impose their own nominee, James Fitzgerald, as head of that great family. Close to the church's entry, a modern plaque marks the place of burial of Aindrias Mac Craith, a Rabelaisian, witty, and very gifted poet of the 18th century. His final verse appears on the plaque, calling on God to forgive his sins and admit him to the great 'fortress' of heaven.

The De Valera Museum

Bruree, County Limerick

Éamon de Valera was born of a Spanish father and an Irish mother in New York in 1882. His father died three years later, and the little boy was sent to Ireland by his mother to be reared by her people in Bruree. They were poor, but made every effort to get a good education for their intelligent young charge. He won a scholarship to Blackrock College in Dublin, and later received a degree in mathematics and became a teacher. He took part in the Rising of 1916, being commander of the company which took over Boland's Bakery in Dublin in an attempt to prevent British reinforcements from reaching the city centre. Sentenced to death, he was reprieved and later made a dramatic escape from prison in England, after which he became President of Sinn Féin and was a leading member of the first Dáil Éireann. Because he refused to accept the Treaty of 1922, he was excluded from government in the Irish Free State.

In 1926, de Valera founded a new party, Fianna Fáil, and by 1933 he was the premier or Taoiseach (literally 'chieftain') of the Irish Government. He followed moderate populist policies, and he and his party dominated Irish politics for the next generation. From 1959 to 1973 he was Uachtarán, or president, of Ireland. He died in 1975, but the heritage of de Valera still looms large in the debate concerning national identity, and his folk image is that of a resourceful and witty, if somewhat austere, figure. In his socio-cultural vision, de Valera was much influenced by his rural background, and would be particularly proud of the little museum dedicated to him in the town of his childhood.

Sybil Point
County Kerry

Piaras Feiritéar was a nobleman and poet whose castle overlooked the sea on Sybil Head, at the extreme west of the Dingle Peninsula. He fought against the Cromwellian forces from the beginning of hostilities in 1641, and continued the fighting when the rest of the country had surrendered. Finally, in 1653, he was invited to a parley by the enemy and, despite being promised safe passage, was treacherously seized and brought to Killarney, where he was hanged on Fair Hill.

Because of his colourful poetry and his great courage, Piaras is remembered as a dashing hero. He was a great horseman – having seven fine stallions – and he delighted in gambling, card-playing and riddle-contests. During his guerrilla campaign against the English soldiers, he made several daring escapes. Once, when a large body of Roundheads surrounded the castle, he had a false bridge constructed over a sea-cleft nearby. He then feigned a retreat, and the enemy forces rushed headlong in pursuit over the bridge, only to fall into the sea far below. When sore pressed, he retired to the Great Blasket island, a few miles off the coast, and hid in a cave perched perilously high on the cliffs. A fanciful story explains the placename Sybil Point by claiming that he once sailed north to Galway, and that a young noblewoman called Sybil Lynch eloped with him from there. Her father in great anger sent a strong naval force to take her back, and Piaras decided to hide her in a cave facing the sea near his castle while he drew them off by a feint. Before he could return to her, however, she was drowned by a sudden and massive sea-wave.

Ross Castle

County Kerry

The greater Lake of Killarney is known as *Loch Léin*, and jutting out into its centre is Ross Island. Here stand the ruins of the fine castle of Ó Donnchú Mór ('the Great O'Donohoe'), chieftain of the principal line of his sept. The O'Donohoes were on this site since the early Middle Ages, but the huge tower and the small bailey date from the 15th century. The castle – which originally consisted of four floors – was attacked by a large Cromwellian army in 1652, and heavy bombardment from the land and from floating batteries on the water reduced it to its present state. The long tradition of the O'Donohoes is reflected in many placenames around the lake, so it is not surprising to discover that the whole area is said to be under the mystical protection of the ancestor of that family. He was Dónall Ó Donnchú, a leading figure in 12th-century Ireland, and it is said that his ghost still keeps residence at Ross Castle.

A tiny island to the north of Ross is fancifully called 'O'Donohoe's Prison', and so the great ancestor is known by the nickname *Dónall na nGeimhleach* ('Dónall of the Captives'). The actual lore concerning him, however, has him as a liberating figure. He appears every May morning, riding a fine mare along the waters of the lake, and is always available to help people in distress. On one occasion he gave money to tenants who were being persecuted for rents by a local landlord. Having given receipts to the tenants, the landlord found to his dismay that the money turned to leaves. Dónall is also said to be an expert hurler and footballer, and he has often appeared to assist local teams when they were facing defeat in games.

Recreated
Bogland Village
Glenbeigh, County Kerry

Almost a fifth of the surface of Ireland was traditionally covered by peat-bogs, which developed thousands of years ago in waterlogged terrain during periods of cold climate. They consist of successive layers of withered plants and mosses which have combined and consolidated. Many generations of Irish people have extracted turf from these bogs, using varieties of a one-sided spade called a *sleán*. In the early summer, neighbours grouped together to cut the turf in co-operation, and such 'a day on the bog' could be a great social occasion. After cutting, the turf-sods were spread out and then 'footed' (i.e., put leaning together to dry), and at the end of summer they were brought home in baskets hung on either side of the back of a pony or donkey. Each family would then have its own turf-stack near the house, in readiness for use as domestic fuel during the long cold winter nights. Sometimes, too, the bogs might yield up something more exotic, such as fine metal weapons or boxes of butter which had been secreted there long before – for preservation, or perhaps even in sacrifice to spirits of the landscape.

In 1946, *Bord na Móna* ('the peat board') was set up for the purpose of producing fuel on a large scale and through mechanised techniques. A number of processing stations were established, which developed varieties of product such as sod peat, moss peat, milled peat, and briquettes. In this way, the bogs of Ireland met much of the country's needs, providing fuel for domestic and industrial use and even for generating electricity. Large tracts of land, from which the turf had been extracted, were reclaimed for pasture and crops.

Kenmare Bay
County Kerry

According to mythology, the Gaelic people took possession of Ireland from the divine race called Tuatha Dé Danann ('people of the goddess Danu'). The newcomers were led by the sons of a dead champion called Míl, and they approached the country from the south-west. One of these sons of Míl was a poet and wizard, and his name was Amhairghin ('wondrous conception'). He was the first to land and, as he set foot upon the soil of Ireland at Kenmare Bay, he chanted a magical poem of great power. This – in translation from the Irish – is his poem:

> *I am the wind on the sea, a strong wave on the land;*
> *the noise of the sea, and a stag with seven antler-tips;*
> *I am a hawk on a cliff, a drop of sundew, the beauty of growth;*
> *I am a wild boar in courage, a salmon in a pool, a lake on the*
> *   plain;*
> *I am a wizard of knowledge, a victorious javelin slaying in*
> *   battle;*
> *I am a god who kindles inspiration in the head!*
>
> *Who is he that levels the stones on a mountain?*
> *Who is he that computes the seasons of the moon?*
> *To whom is known where the sun sets?*
>
> *Call the druid so that he will sing a charm for ye*
> *- I am the druid, I am the wind on the sea!*

In this way and with these words Amhairghin claimed the new land, not only for himself and his people, but for visionaries and mystics for all time.

The inlet where – according to tradition – the first Irish poem was composed.

Gougane Barra
County Cork

Several ancient monastic foundations in coastal parts of Ireland, and even in Scotland, are attributed to a saint called Barra or Fionnbharra. His name meant 'the white-crested one', and old texts claim that he rode a mysterious horse on the sea and plucked fish from that 'watery plain'. His hand was radiant, and it was said that on his death the sun stood still in the heavens for twelve days. Was Barra, then, a sea-deity or a sky-deity recast in Christian form? The real explanation may be that the name which he bore had resonances of pre-Christian belief, and that his cult was spread far and wide by monks who were devoted to him.

St. Barra seems to have lived in the 6th century, and to have been an accomplished scholar. Finding a little island on a deep lake in the Derrynasaggart Mountains, he settled there. The place was called *Gúgán*, meaning 'crevice', and there Barra established a famous school for clerics. The river Lee rises at this 'Gougane Barra' and, after some time, an angel directed the saint to follow the course of that river as it flowed directly eastward for 50 miles (80 kilometres). It went through marshland before entering the sea, and at that place Barra founded a hermitage. Many people flocked there, forming a settlement which grew into Cork city. Far to the west, however, his little foundation at Gougane had a mystique all of its own. A little causeway leads out onto the island, on which the ruins of an old chapel and a holy well stand among luxuriant trees. Many people still go there on pilgrimage, especially on the feast-day of the saint, September 25.

The Old Head of Kinsale
County Cork

The placename of this promontory, in Irish *Cionn tSáile*, is very appropriate, meaning 'the headland on the sea'. Jutting out of the southern coast onto the Atlantic Ocean, it has been for centuries a point of great importance in travel between Ireland and the European continent. The highest part of the head rises to over 260 feet (80 metres), and has the remains of a signal station erected as part of the elaborate system of coastal protections against a threatened invasion by Napoleon. There are also a light-house and the ruins of a late mediaeval castle.

Historical events of major importance took place to either side of the Old Head. The town of Kinsale, which takes its name from the headland, lies some 10 miles (15 kilometres) to the north, scene of the tragic conclusion to the 'Nine Years War', a campaign by the Ulster chieftains to regain Irish independence. After a Spanish relief force was blockaded by the English army in Kinsale towards the end of the year 1601, the northern forces led by Aodh Ó Néill, Aodh Rua Ó Dónaill, and Walter Tyrrell had no choice but to march southwards to the relief. The plan was to attack the English at dawn of Christmas Eve, so taking them unawares, but everything went wrong. The Irish forces wandered about all night in the boglands, lashed by rainstorms, and to their consternation found the English army ready and waiting in the morning. The resultant rout was the prelude to centuries of untrammelled English rule in Ireland. A long time later, and at a similar distance from the Old Head – in the Atlantic to the south – a German submarine torpedoed and sank the *Lusitania* in 1915. This began a chain of events which eventually led to the entry of the USA into the First World War.

The 'Moving Statue' at Ballinspittle

County Cork

The Irish people have always had a special devotion to the Virgin Mary. Many songs told of her desolation and unbearable sorrow as she saw her son Jesus put to death, and she has always been regarded as a special sympathiser in times of misfortune and as a refuge for those in despair. There is therefore a long tradition of communicating with Mary in personal prayer. In overt custom, however, the large array of local Irish saints – both male and female – have predominated, with the result that Marian devotion in terms of processions and statues has not been as marked in Ireland as in other European countries.

All of this changed in recent centuries, with the promotion of the image of Mary as 'Queen of Heaven'. In 1832 she was said to have appeared to a man in Charleville, County Cork, warning of a cholera epidemic. Then there were the famous apparitions at Knock in County Mayo in 1879, and the less influential reports of appearances of the Virgin in 1939 at Kerrytown, County Donegal. Pilgrimages to the great centres of Marian devotion abroad increased through the 20th century, and one widespread tradition of southern Europe gradually gained currency in Ireland – the cult of statues. There were sporadic reports of these showing signs of life, and a particularly controversial case at Templemore, County Tipperary, in 1920, concerned a 'bleeding' statue. The greatest stir of all was caused, however, in the late summer of 1985, when statues of Mary over a wide area – particularly in Munster – were said to be moving and shedding tears. Large crowds gathered to pray at these statues, most notably at one in a village south-west of Kinsale. This village inherited a caring name from olden times, *Baile an Spidéil* (literally, 'town of the hospital').

Although the custom of congregating at 'moving' statues died away almost as quickly as it had begun in 1985, a dwindling number of people continue their devotion to this one at Ballinspittle.

Blarney Castle
County Cork

A chieftain of the MacCarthys, called Cormac Láidir ('strong Cormac'), was a great builder, and the most striking of his works was Blarney Castle, which dates from the year 1446. With a massive square keep and a battlemented parapet over 80 feet (25 metres) above the ground, it stands on a rock over the river Croomaun, 5 miles (8 kilometres) to the north-west of Cork city. The MacCarthys managed to keep control of the castle through tumultuous times, until it was finally taken from them by the English Government. The poet Aogán Ó Rathaille (1670-1728) lamented the fact that the castle, bartered from one settler to another, had become 'a dwelling-place for wolves'.

The toponymic Blarney – in Irish *Blarna* – means 'expansive place', due to the fine view to be had there. In recent times, however, it has acquired an additional and humorous meaning. This is connected with the tourist custom of 'kissing the Blarney stone' in order to get the gift of eloquent speech. The flagstone in question is situated just below the battlements of the castle, and one must lie down and reach backwards to kiss it, but the origin of the custom is obscure. It is said that the MacCarthy chieftain in the early 17th century tried to postpone his surrender to the English by using 'fair words and soft speech', thereby causing Queen Elizabeth I to declare that 'this is all Blarney!'. The MacCarthys did, indeed, have great respect for good speech, having been patrons of the Gaelic poets for centuries. For some generations after their demise, groups of poets continued to meet periodically in the village beside the castle, thus bolstering the reputation of the place for learning and eloquence.

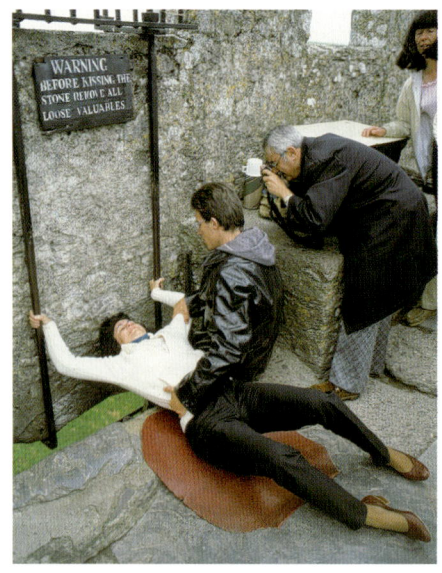

Horse-fair at Cahirmee
County Cork

The horse was the most valuable animal in traditional Ireland, and accordingly many folk beliefs and superstitions centred on it. As well as sickness and injury, other dangers threatened the horse, for it was thought that an envious neighbour could harm it by a glance of 'the evil eye' or that the fairies might wish to spirit it away into the otherworld, leaving only a useless nag in its place. In order to protect it from such misfortunes, a red ribbon or a twig of rowan might be attached to its mane while it was in the stable, or one might spit on it before releasing it into the field.

Much of the lore of horses can be learned by attending a horse-fair. Good luck is sealed into a bargain, for instance, by spitting on the palms before the handshake, and the seller should always retain the halter so as to preserve his good luck. There are many maxims concerning the colours and markings of horses, some thought to be good portents and others bad, but people seldom agree on all of these. One very old way of judging the best qualities of a horse goes as follows: 'Three traits of a bull – bold walk, strong neck, and hard hoof; three traits of a hare – light ear, slanting eye, and quick turn; three traits of a woman – broad breast, slender waist, and short back!' One of the best-known traditional horse-fairs is held annually at Cahirmee, halfway between the towns of Buttevant and Doneraile in County Cork. Many a good farmhorse, pony, and hunter were bought at this fair, including – it is said – the charger ridden by the Duke of Wellington at the Battle of Waterloo. According to another tradition, Napoleon's famous horse, Marengo, was bred in County Wexford!

Tountinna
County Tipperary

Overlooking Lough Derg, on the east bank of the river Shannon a few miles from the town of Portroe, is the hill known as Tountinna (in Irish *Tul Toinne*, 'prominence over water'). Within that hill, according to tradition, the seer Fionntan spent many years during the great deluge, he being the only survivor of that disaster in Ireland. The story occurs in a mediaeval compilation which combines native mythology, classical learning, and no small degree of fiction. Fionntan himself bears a shamanic name, derived from a Celtic *Vindosenos* meaning 'enlightened old man', and he bears the patronymic Mac Bóchna ('son of the sea'). The Christian writers naturally seized the opportunity of connecting him with the great flood mentioned in the Old Testament, and so this extraordinary tradition grew up.

It was claimed that Fionntan as a youth was one of an antediluvian group of three men and fifty women who came to settle in Ireland. The two other men died, and Fionntan – being the sole male survivor – felt overwhelmed by the fond attentions of the women. He therefore fled from them and went to hide within the hill of Tountinna. The deluge came then, but Fionntan remained in his insulated refuge until the great inundation had passed. His skill at survival continued, and it was said that he lived for thousands of years more, passing from the shape of a salmon into an eagle, and finally a falcon, before returning to human shape at the time when Christianity came to Ireland. He knew all the ancient lore of the country, and was therefore in great demand as a storyteller at the court of the High-King in Tara. Worn out by his multiple years, he finally expired near Kenmare in County Kerry.

Mount Bruis
Shronell, County Tipperary

Joseph Damer was a banker and entrepreneur who moved from England to Dublin in 1662 and soon purchased large tracts of land in County Tipperary from the Cromwellian settlers. He filled these lands with sheep and set up a vast business in the export of wool. Though phenomenally rich, Joseph was reputed to have been a miser – Dean Swift wrote that 'he walked the streets and wore a threadbare cloak, he dined and supped at charge of other folk'. He died unmarried in 1720, and the massive wealth passed to his nephew John.

Like his uncle, John Damer was also said to have been very careful with his money, and several stories are told about this. In the year 1740 he commenced the building of a great mansion in Shronell, on a little hill which he called Mount Bruis. It was said that he had a secret vaulted room in that mansion, with the doors heavily padlocked, and that he had a vast treasure in sovereigns hidden away there. A travelling tailor came by one day and offered to cut a new suit of clothes for Damer. The magnate quickly enquired as to the cost, and the tailor answered that the only payment he desired was one look at the treasure. Damer was very pleased at this, and when the work was done they went to observe the glittering sovereigns. Growing curious, Damer asked the tailor what could he gain from this, and received the quick reply: 'It does me the same good, sir, as it does yourself!' The gable is all that now remains of the great house at Shronell. It is said that there were 365 windows in that house, one for every day in the year!

Crotty's Rock

County Waterford

At a height of nearly 2,625 feet (800 metres) in the Comeragh Mountains there are several remote places which are said to have served as hideouts for a celebrated outlaw called Liam Ó Crotaigh (William Crotty). The best known lies between the lakes of Coumgaura and Coumshingaun, it being a rock ledge underneath which is a deep declivity forming a type of broad chamber. This is known as *Stolla Chrotaigh* or 'Crotty's Rock'. The hideout is almost inaccessible, and can be entered only by lowering oneself perilously on a rope.

The epitome of a noble-minded outlaw, Crotty (1712-1742) was the son of a poor farmer who was evicted from his holding in Russelstown, south of Clonmel, by a tyrannical landlord. At the age of eighteen, he gathered together a group of other young men and they played the role of folk heroes by 'robbing the rich to help the poor'. They frequented the Comeragh Mountains, from which they descended to carry out raids on the landlords and their associates, and then melted back into the mountains again out of the reach of the numerous troops of soldiers sent to apprehend them. Crotty himself is said to have been an accomplished sportsman and dancer. His faithful wife was Mary Norris, from the village of Curraheen, and her brother David was his right-hand man. It is said that Mary suspected the loyalty of her brother, and she was proved correct in the end, for David's wife betrayed Crotty to the soldiers and David himself swore evidence against him. Crotty was hanged in Waterford, but his ghost has often been seen in the Comeragh Mountains, mounted on a white horse and guarding his hidden treasure.

Wren-Boys
(various counties)

In olden times, the advance of winter would have suggested to people that the cold and misery were being brought on by a hostile spirit. The wren is the tiniest bird in this clime. It flies closest to the ground and makes its nest in the earth. Thus it was easy for people to imagine that this bird impeded the vegetation and represented the spirit of winter. To bring the winter to an end, a ritual of hunting the wren was common in western Europe in the Middle Ages.

The earliest report of the wren-hunt in Ireland is in a fanciful mediaeval biography of Moling, a famous saint of old. We read that Moling kept as pets in his monastic cell a wren and a fly. The wren killed the fly, whereupon the saint cursed that bird, saying, 'Let his dwelling be forever in empty houses, and may there be always a wet drip there, and may children and rabble be slaughtering him!' An increased humanitarian sense among the people meant that there was a gradual shift from killing an actual wren to replacing it with an effigy, and often to a mere claim that the wren had been hunted. And so, in many parts of Ireland, on the morning of St. Stephen's Day (December 26), groups of youngsters go in fantastic disguise from house to house playing music and singing verses such as:

> *The wren, the wren, the king of all birds*
> *on St. Stephen's Day was caught in the furze;*
> *although he is little, his family is great*
> *– so rise up, landlady, and give us a treat!*

Wren-boys at Dingle, County Kerry.

Picture Credits

Index

A

Ailill, king 17

Aill Bhuí, Ballyvaughan 99

Amhairghin 120

Ardee, County Louth 69

Ardnacrusha, County Clare 25

Armada 103

Armagh, County 94

Athlone, County Westmeath 66

Avondale House, County Wicklow 34

B

Balar, king 77

Ballingarry, County Limerick 107

Ballinspittle, County Cork 127

Ballyneety, County Limerick 108

Barra (saint) 123

Blackstairs Mountains, Counties
    Wexford and Carlow 38

Blarney Castle, County Cork 128

Blarney stone 128

Bod Fhearghusa 65

Bogland Village, Glenbeigh, County
    Kerry 119

Bóinn (goddess) 62

Book of Armagh 100

Bord na Móna (peat board) 119

bowling 94

Boyne, Battle of the 85

Boyne, River 62, 85

Brian Boru 100

Bricriu 89

Broaders, Fr Thomas 42

Bruree, County Limerick 112

Burke, Sir Richard 17

Burke, Theobald 17

Burren, County Clare 99

Butler, Piaras Rua, Earl of Ormond 37

Butler, Margaret 37

C

Cahirmee, County Cork 131

Canair (holy lady) 104

Cappawhite, County Tipperary 74

carols 41

Cattle-Raid of Cooley 69, 89

Cave Hill, County Antrim 82

Ceallóg (holy man) 111

Cessair 74

Charleville, County Cork 127

Christchurch, Dublin 54

Clare Island, County Mayo 18

Clonkeen, County Kildare 62

Clontarf, Battle of 100

coirm 45

Coleraine, County Derry 73

Collegiate Church, Kilmallock, County
    Limerick 111

Comeragh Mountains, County
    Waterford 136

Conchobhar, king of Ulster 89

Connachta tribe 81

Cork, County 94

Croke Park, Dublin 50

Cromwellian Wars 115

Crotty, William 136

Crotty's Rock, County Waterford 136

Cruachain 17

Cú Chulainn 69, 89

Cualainn tribe 33

Cuilcagh Mountains 25

curachs 21

Currach 30

Custume, Sergeant 66

D

Daghdha (deity) 33

Dáil Éireann 57, 112

Dál gCais sept 100

Damer, John 135

Damer, Joseph 135

Dawson, Sir Joshua 57

de Clare, Richard 'Strongbow', Earl of
    Pembroke 54

de Valera, Éamon 112

de Valera Museum, Bruree, County
    Limerick 112

Dergh, Lough 132

Devereux, Fr William 41

Dingle, County Kerry 139

Donn (god) 107

drama 93

Draperstown, County Derry 74

Drogheda, County Louth 62

Dublin
    Castle 53
    Christchurch 54
    Grand Canal 26
    Guinness Brewery 61
    Mansion House 57
public houses 45
    St. Enda's Museum 58

Dún Dá Bheann 73

Dundrum Bay, County Down 86

E

Easter Rising 58, 112

Elizabeth I, queen of England 18,
    103, 128

Elizabethan Wars 82

Emmet, Robert 53

F

Fear Dia 69

Feiritéar, Piaras 115

Fethard-on-Sea, County Wexford 42

Fianna Fáil 112

Fionnbharra 107, 123

Fionntan 132

Fir Deadhadh tribe 69

fishing 78
Fitzgerald, Gearóid Mór, Earl of Kildare 37
Fitzgerald, Gearóid Óg, Earl of Kildare 37
Fitzgerald, James Fitzmaurice 111
Fitzgerald, 'Silken' Thomas 53
Fleadh Cheoil na hÉireann 22
Fomhoire deities 77

G
Gaelic football 94
Gaelic League 58
Galway hookers 21
George IV, king of England 57
Ginkel, General 66
Glenbeigh, County Kerry 119
Gougane Barra, County Cork 123
Gráinne Mhaol 18
Grand Canal, Dublin 26
Great Blasket Island 115
Great Sugarloaf, County Wicklow 33
Greencastle, County Down 74
Guinness, Arthur 61
Guinness Brewery, Dublin 61

H
Henry II, king of England 54
High-kings of Ireland 65, 81, 100
Holy Well, County Clare 96
hookers (sailing boats) 21
horses
    racing 30, 65
    sales 74, 131
hurling 50, 94

I
Inniskeen, County Monaghan 90
Irish Republican Brotherhood 58

J
James II, king of England 66, 85
Johnson, Esther 46

K
Kavanagh, Patrick 90

Kavanagh Museum, County Monaghan 90
Kenmare Bay, County Kerry 120
Kerrytown, County Donegal 127
Keshcorran, County Sligo 14
Killaloe, County Clare 100
Killarney, Lake of 116
Killorglin, County Kerry 74
Killybegs Harbour, County Donegal 78
Kilmallock, County Limerick 111
Kilmore Quay, County Wexford 41
Kincora, County Clare 100
Kinsale, County Cork 124
Knock, County Mayo 127
Knockfeerina, County Limerick 107

L
Land League 34
Leinster, Mount 38
Leixlip, County Kildare 61
Lia Fáil Stone, County Meath 65
Limerick 25, 108
Loftus, Anne 42
Loftus Hall, County Wexford 42
Loughbrickland, County Down 89
Lua (saint) 100
Lugh (god) 30, 77
Lusitania 124
Lynch, Sybil 115

M
Mac Airt, Cormac 14
Mac Craith, Aindrias 111
Mac Cuarta, Séamas 90
Mac Cumhaigh, Art 90
Mac Cumhaill, Fionn 14, 62, 74
Mac Bóchna, Fionntan 132
Mac Fhlannchadha, Baothghalach 103
Mac Léide, Fearghus 86
Mac Morna, Goll 14
Mac Murchadha, Diarmaid 54
MacArt's Fort, County Antrim 82
MacCarthy, Cormac Ládir 128
Madagán, king of Ulster 82
Mansion House, Dublin 57
Mathghamhain 100

McClancy, Boethius 103
Meadhbh (goddess) 17
Meadhbh, queen of Connacht 66, 69
Mesolithic people 73
Míl (mythic champion) 120
Moling (saint) 139
Mount Bruis, Shronell, County Tipperary 135
Mountjoy, Lord Deputy 82
Mountsandel, County Derry 73
Mullinavat, County Kilkenny 74
mumming 70, 93
music 22, 41, 93

N
Napoleon I 131
Nath Í 17
New York, USA 49
Niall, king of Tara 17, 81
Nine Years War 81, 124
Norris, Mary 136

O
Ó Crotaigh, Liam 136
Ó Doirnín, Peadar 90
Ó Dónaill, Aodh Rua 53, 124
Ó Donnchú, Dónall 116
Ó Donnchú Mór 116
Ó hÓgáin, Dónall 108
Ó Neill, Aodh, Earl of Dungannon 81, 124
Ó Neill, Brian Mac Airt 82
Ó Rathaille, Aogán 128
O'Connor kings 17
O'Donohue sept 116
Oileán Toraí 77
Oímelg festival 29
Old Head of Kinsale, County Cork 124
Oldbridge, County Meath 85
O'Malley clan 18
Orange Order 85
Orange Parade, County Down 85
O'Shea, Kitty 34

P
Pallasgreen, County Limerick 108

Parnell, Charles Stewart 34
Pearse, Pádraic 58
peat-digging 119
Perrott, Sir John 111
public houses 45
Punchestown, County Kildare 30

R
Rathcroghan, County Roscommon 17
Rathdrum, County Wicklow 34
Ross Castle, County Kerry 116
Rossa, Jeremiah O'Donovan 58
Rossport, County Mayo 12
Rudhraighe tribe 86

S
St. Barra 123
St. Brigid 29, 54
St. Brigid's Cathedral, Kildare 29
St. Canice's Cathedral, Kilkenny 37
St. Enda's Museum, Dublin 58
St. Moling 139
St. Patrick's Cathedral, Dublin 46
St. Patrick's Day Parade, Dublin 49

St. Ruth, Maréchal 66
St. Stephen's Day 139
San Esteban (ship) 103
San Marcos (ship) 103
Sarsfield, Patrick 108
Scattery Island, County Clare 104
Seanán (saint) 104
shamrock 49
Shannon, River 25, 66, 104
sheep 74
Shronell, County Tipperary 135
Sinn Féin 112
Sliabh Chualann 33
Spanish Point, County Clare 103
'Strongbow' 54
Swift, Jonathan 46, 135
Sybil Point, County Kerry 115

T
Tara, County Meath 81, 132
    Hill of 65
Templemore, County Tipperary 127
Tone, Theobald Wolfe 82
Tory Island, County Donegal 77

Tottenham, Honourable Charles 42
Tountinna, County Tipperary 132
Tuatha Dé Danann 65, 77, 120
Tullaghogue, County Tyrone 81
Tyrrell, Walter 124

U
Uí Néill family 81
United Irishmen 82, 85
United States of America 49, 124

V
Virgin Mary 127

W
Waddinge, Fr Luke 41
War of Independence 57
War of the Two Kings 66
Wellington, Duke of 131
West, Benjamin 85
William III, king of England 66, 85, 108
World War I 124
wren-boys 139